HEAD-ON COLLISION WITH GOD

From DUI to Divinely Used Instrument

RODNEY WRIGHT

Largo, MD

Copyright © 2022 Rodney Wright

All rights reserved under the international copyright law. No part of this book may be reproduced or transmitted in any form or by any means, electronic or mechanical, including photocopying, recording, or by any information storage and retrieval system, without the express, written permission of the publisher or the author. The exception is reviewers, who may quote brief passages in a review.

Christian Living Books, Inc.
We bring your dreams to fruition.
P.O. Box 7584
Largo, MD 20792
ChristianLivingBooks.com

ISBN 9781562295745

Unless otherwise indicated, Scripture taken from the New King James Version®. Copyright © 1982 by Thomas Nelson. Used by permission. All rights reserved. Scripture quotations marked (NIV) are taken from the Holy Bible, New International Version®, NIV®. Copyright © 1973, 1978, 1984, 2011 by Biblica, Inc.® Used by permission of Zondervan. All rights reserved worldwide.

DEDICATION

I dedicate this book to the two young men who lost their lives in this tragic accident and to their family and friends. I think about you every single day of my life. You will never fully know how truly sorry I am. I hope you can see this book as just one of the many things I will do to keep my word to do what you requested of me.

This book is also dedicated to all the people who have lost loved ones due to accidents caused by drivers under the influence. My heart goes out to you all. I hope these writings make a difference and reduce lives lost in the future.

CONTENTS

Acknowledgments   vii
Special Acknowledgment   ix
Introduction   xi

Section 1: Growing Up – Egypt   1
   Chapter 1 – Relationship with My Parents   3
   Chapter 2 – Rodney vs. Automatik   7
   Chapter 3 – Love for Basketball   25
   Chapter 4 – Auto the MC   33
   Chapter 5 – Home Life   37

Section 2: The Accident – Exodus at the Red Sea   45
   Chapter 6 – The Spiral   47
   Chapter 7 – The Collision   53
   Chapter 8 – My Injuries   59
   Chapter 9 – The Arrest   65

Section 3: Prison – The Wilderness   67
   Chapter 10 – Processing   69
   Chapter 11 – Life in the Thunderdome – 2400 Block   71
   Chapter 12 – 5200 – The School Dorm   81
   Chapter 13 – Acceptance and Accountability   87
   Chapter 14 – The Court Proceedings and Final Sentencing   99
   Chapter 15 – Epiphanies in Prison   103

Section 4: Purpose and New Outlook on Life: The Promised Land   123
   Chapter 16 – Reentry and the System   125
   Chapter 17 – The First Year out of Prison   129
   Chapter 18 – Peace Is the Greatest Accomplishment   143

Epilogue   153
About the Author   155

ACKNOWLEDGMENTS

Praise and all glory to my Father in heaven, YAHWEH, my God. Thank You for saving me time and time again. To my Lord and Savior Jesus Christ, thank You for paying the price I couldn't pay and interceding for me constantly. Through You, my loved ones and I have salvation.

To my wife, Totteanna Wright, thank you for being my better half. Thank you for standing by me, supporting me, and keeping me sane during the worst time of my life. Thank you for waiting for hours in those dirty jail waiting rooms to see me for thirty minutes through that thick glass. Thank you for spending countless nights sleeping on couches in my hospital rooms just so I wouldn't feel alone. You are the reason why I made it through. You are definitely heaven-sent.

To my daughters, De'jah, Lyric, Kennedy, and Emory, I love you, and I'm sorry for my missteps and the pain I caused you. To Zai, thank you for talking to me about the Bible stories you learned during our visits. Thank you to my mother-in-law, Tish, and Aunt Earline for being the mother I didn't have, but needed, during this horrible time of my life. I will never forget that. Thank you to Nicky Orr for driving two-and-a-half hours to come to my court dates to support me and for helping with the "man" things in my household while I was gone.

Thank you to my father and Brianne for the financial assistance while I was in jail. You were the only people I could count on in that area while I was gone, and that is big. Thank you to my sister Monica for taking turns with Tottie sleeping in my hospital rooms. I don't remember much from the hospital, but I remember that you were there when I needed you and I'll never forget that. Also thank you for coming to court dates and for keeping Kennedy close to our side of the family. That was big! Thank you to my sister Bri for the visits. You are one of my heroes. Thank you, Nonnie, for always being a loving grandmother to me and making me feel special. Your house was always a place of refuge for me. Thank you to my grandmother Allura for allowing me the time to rebuild. You are the reason I was able to buy my properties. Thank you, Roston, for the visits and words of encouragement when I needed them. You didn't know it, but they were right on time and ordained by God. Thank you to my brother Eric for the letters, pictures, and continued support. You are a true brother. Thank you to my brothers Alluron and Matt for taking time out to come to visit me. That was "stand-up," and I'll never forget it. Thank you to my brother SB for picking me up from the rehabilitation home and pushing me around in the wheelchair. You didn't know at the time but that made me feel normal for a brief but critical moment in time. Also thank you for the support at the court dates and for always being the voice of reason. Thank you to Trenisha, Roy, Tracy, and everybody who came to support me during court dates.

Special Acknowledgment

To my brother, Quamé, the inspiration, editor, and pretty much the co-author of this book. I don't have the words to say how much I appreciate you. This started as a friend calling to check on a friend who went through a tough time, but it turned into somewhat of a counseling/therapy session,
which turned into a book.
This was your idea.
You are a genius
and a visionary.
This was therapy.
You helped save my
life and you didn't
even know it.
Thank you, bro!

Quamé 2022

INTRODUCTION

As a kid, I was never much of a reader or writer. I wasn't interested in writing anything but rap. So, I never thought in a million years I would author a book.

Growing up, I was so ashamed of my parents and home life. I became a master at hiding and disguising my reality, feelings, faults, and the authentic me. *Head-On Collision with God* is the true story of a kid who was traumatized due to his childhood plagued by addiction, gang violence, and generational curses. He grew to be a double-minded man with a chip on his shoulder disguised as a churchgoer/company-man by day and a rapper/street dude by night. Eventually, these two personas collided on one fatal night in 2017 when a head-on collision left two people dead and one clinging to life in ICU.

This book is about my life journey and true experiences with God. It is parallel to the Israelites' (God's chosen people) deliverance and journey from Egypt, the land of bondage and slavery, through the wilderness to the Promised Land. The Israelites' story is captured in the book of Exodus in the Bible.

This is a narrative about trauma, anxiety, addiction, arrogance, self-accountability, deliverance, spirituality, the failed prison and judicial system, depression, and the lack of awareness in the Black community. It is a cautionary tale of what can happen when one of God's sheep strays too far from the Shepherd. I hope that you enjoy reading, but most importantly, that you learn and grow from its contents even more.

SECTION 1

GROWING UP IN MY WORLD: EGYPT

CHAPTER 1

RELATIONSHIP WITH MY PARENTS

QUAMÉ: I would love to know more about your parents from your memory as a youth to now. What were they like personality-wise? What was life like with them? When did you learn about their addiction? Can you remember your initial reaction?

Rodney: My parents were not very good at parenting. But at this point, I realize they weren't supposed to be. They had me when they were 15 and 17 years old.

They were just kids learning their way. Of course, they were going to make big mistakes. My mother has always been a mouthy, disrespectful woman and would be this way to any spouse. Honestly, she got it from her mother, Nonnie, who is my heart. My mother is from "The Bottoms," a known ghetto part of Inglewood, California off 104th and Crenshaw Boulevard. My father is from Inglewood but on the north side of Century Blvd where the houses are and the more affluent, hard-working Black people live. So, of course, when my father's mother found out that her promising, borderline genius son got this little "Bottoms" girl from the "other side" of Inglewood pregnant, she was not happy.

My parents' relationship was volatile from the start. They were always arguing and fighting. I didn't realize drug use was involved until I was 7 years old. That's when I noticed something was wrong. My parents would be locked in the bathroom for hours, only to come out periodically with big eyes, paranoid, and constantly checking the windows. Nobody ever told me what they were doing. I figured it out on my own. I remember watching Public Enemy's video, "Night of the Living Baseheads," and the crack addicts looked just like my parents did at home. That was my confirmation. It was a crushing and embarrassing revelation. Think about it; both of your parents are crackheads, baseheads, dope-fiends–what the kids at school talked about in their jokes. It was horrible, and I did not want anybody to find out.

My parents, George and Lanell, at the Loyola High School prom – 1977

My parents at Club Players Choice – 1986

QUAMÉ: Where are your parents now? Are they still together?

Rodney: My parents were never married. They split up when I was 19 years old. My father lives in Santa Clarita, about ten minutes away from me. He's doing very well. He got off of crack when I was around 20 years old and in college. He completely turned his life around. He is now an executive at a well known communications company.

He has three more children from his partner of over twenty years, plus the four he already had (three from my mother and one from a woman before my mother).

On the other hand, my mother is still hooked on crack and is out there on the street. We talk every now and then, but it is never pleasant. Usually, she's asking for money or something. Her addiction drives her, and it is really difficult to deal with, particularly because she is my mother whom I love so much.

My mother is very selfish and hard to deal with. I try not to clash with her too much because she didn't have the best childhood herself, and I understand she has unresolved issues. My mother is the product of a broken marriage. She is Nonnie's second oldest child, but the firstborn of the children from Nonnie's marriage to my biological grandfather, Lionel Reagor Sr. My grandparents were married and living what seemed to be a happy life. Lionel Sr. was a professional man who worked for Pacific Bell. He and Nonnie bought a home in an affluent Black neighborhood at the time. For whatever reason, one day, Lionel Sr. did not come home from work. He went missing for weeks. It was discovered that he had a mistress. He ended up leaving Nonnie for this woman, married her, and had more children. They moved to a more affluent neighborhood and had productive lives. Contrarily, Nonnie and her children's (three with him) quality of life dropped because her ex-husband refused to support them. He showed little interest in their lives once the divorce was final.

I'm not passing judgment because I understand I am only getting one side of the story. He recently passed away, so I will probably never get his side. But what I can say is my mother was very attached to him. She was considered a daddy's girl before the split. I believe the issues she has today have a lot to do with the abandonment of her father. I wish I knew more about the situation, but what I can say is we have lived in the same city with my grandfather (before his death) my whole life, and I have only seen him once or twice. Knowing her back story, I now feel more compassion for my mother than anything else, but it doesn't make dealing with her any easier.

I seldom see my parents. Since getting out of jail, I've seen my father three times, and those were all brief encounters. My father is super concerned about COVID-19. I haven't seen my mother at all.

CHAPTER 2

RODNEY VS. AUTOMATIK

QUAMÉ: I originally met you as "Automatik" through your cousin Yung Walt in 2002. Who was Automatik? How would you describe Auto as someone separate from yourself?

Rodney: I am a Gemini, and I've always felt like two people in one. I was a shy kid, but in my element, like on the basketball court, I had no problem standing out. The little, shy kid became an arrogant beast once I got on that court.

I was a smart kid who attended a Catholic school from kindergarten to seventh grade. But at the same time, I grew up in Inglewood, California in an area literally called "The Bottoms" in the late 80s and early 90s. It was the worst possible time in history to live there in the height of the crack era and gangbanging. My family was in the middle of all of those elements.

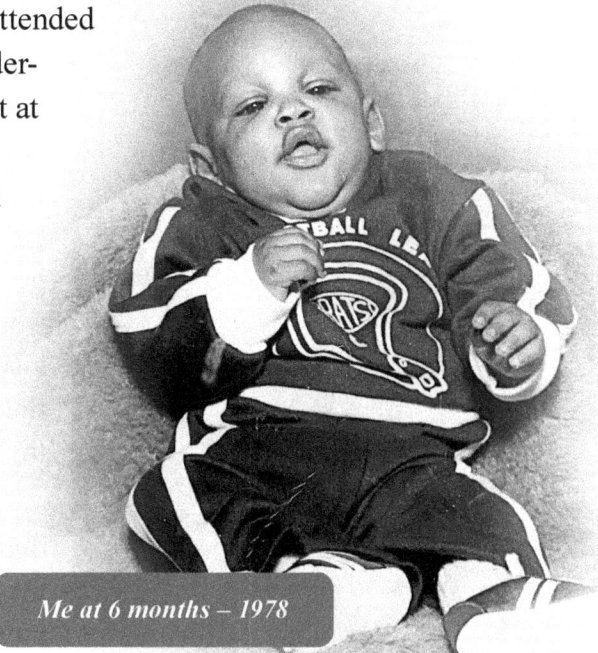

Me at 6 months – 1978

Me in The Bottoms at 2 years old – 1981

Me in pre-school – 1983

I had two role models growing up. One was my father, who was a super smart dude. He was so smart he skipped two grades and graduated from an all-boys, private high school (Loyola High School) at sixteen. I heard he got accepted into MIT. He would always get jobs but would lose them because of his addiction. My other role model was my uncle, PJ (Pimpin' Juny).

He was the hustling street dude on my mother's side of the family. He sold dope, had money and jewelry, and, most importantly, he had the respect of the entire family. When he came by, the world stopped because he was there. He had that aura, that "it" thing people talk about. As I said earlier, I was a shy kid everywhere but on the court, and I wanted *that* aura Juny had. So when basketball didn't work out, I started doing music and a little bit of hustling. I guess I was doing my best "PJ" impression. That's where the name "Automatik" came from. Automatik is a part of me, but a *way* smaller part than I used to let on.

QUAMÉ: Who is Uncle Juny? Please tell us more!

Rodney: Uncle Juny, Lionel Reagor Jr. ("Junior" is where the name "Juny" came from.) and PJ Fly are all the same person. Juny was Inglewood's version of "Money Makin Mitch" from the movie, "Paid In Full." Juny is my mother's little brother. He is the fourth of my grandmother's five children. I named my grandmother Nonnie when I was a baby, but in The Bottoms everybody calls her "Mama Joyce."

Juny is that dude who realized his people were living in poverty and used the only way he

Uncle Juny (aka PJ Fly) at Club Carolina West – 1987

knew to try to get them out. He started selling crack in his early teens like a lot of the young kids at that time and got rich off of it. He used as many people as he could to get to where he needed to be. He was hot-headed and that got him respect. He always had guns. He watched his older brother, Boogie, get murdered in front of him in The Bottoms over a girl.

In 1983, my uncle Boogie, Nonnie's first born and my mother's older brother, went to The Bottoms to visit his mom and show off his new Benz to his little brother Juny. When he pulled up, he saw Juny down the street talking to a girl in front of her house. So, Boogie got out and they were all talking for a while. The girl, in awe of Boogie because of his persona and the fact that he was driving a very expensive car, didn't realize her boyfriend had just pulled up. By the time she realized it, it was too late, and he was parking. He got out of the car obviously upset and expected an explanation. A slight argument took place between the girl, her boyfriend, and Juny. So, of course, older brother had to intervene.

My uncle James (Boogie) Bellinger's obituary – 1983

The story goes that Boogie got kind of disrespectful and told this dude, in front of his girlfriend, "You betta hop your broke ass in your little tonka truck and get from over here

My grandmother Nonnie visiting Juny at the Youth Authority Correctional Camp – 1980

before something happens to you." By the way, the "tonka truck" he was referring to was a very popular Nissan truck at the time in LA, but nothing compared to the Benz Boogie was driving. Anyway, feeling disrespected, the dude left and went to pick up his friend and a gun. He returned, pulled up, fired one shot from the passenger side of his car, and hit Boogie in the head.

Juny held his big brother until the paramedics came, but Boogie died in his arms. This was a drive-by shooting, premeditated murder, right? Well, the story goes the young man's father had recently sued the city of Los Angeles for a work-related injury and won a huge settlement. He used that money to hire a young, charismatic attorney by the name of Johnnie Cochran–made famous by the O.J. Simpson trial–to defend his son. Long story short, the

Juny at Nonnie's house standing on the car he had just bought – 1985

dude who killed my uncle was somehow acquitted on all charges. Most people believe this is what turned Juny into who he became.

I remember on one Fourth of July when I was ten years old, and we were at Alondra Park having a family BBQ. This was the time when dancing was cool. I was dancing in front of everybody. I was constantly looking at Juny for his approval of my dancing. His smiles showed me he was kind of impressed. However, I noticed the expression on his face changed to a cold one as he looked in the direction of the parking lot for about a minute straight. Then out of nowhere, he took off running toward the parking lot super-fast. Nonnie and everybody started screaming, "Juny, what's wrong?"

As he was running, he pulled out a pistol and started firing at a car in the parking lot. All of this happened in a super crowded, Fourth of July, public park. I saw the car he was shooting at spin out

Juny in Lompoc federal prison – 1994

on Artesia Blvd and drive off. Juny hopped in his car and chased after them. After we packed up and left the park, we went to my grandmother's house. When we got there, we saw Juny's car riddled with bullet holes.

Apparently, Juny had spotted Boogie's killer in the parking lot, shot at him, and chased him. They had a shoot-out while racing up Crenshaw. That's the type of dude Juny was–the definition of a street dude. He sold kilos of crack in California and a bunch of other states. Juny was charged with a federal drug trafficking crimes, and he got ten years in federal prison for it. He was also sentenced to twenty years for a murder in Alabama in 1993; those sentences ran concurrently.

He did most of the twenty years and was released around 2012. When Juny got out, I was super excited. It was like the return of the king of LA if you asked me. I thought he was going to pick up right where he left off as far as his grind for "success." I threw him a big party at a popular lounge, got him some clothes, and put a little money in his pocket. However, I experienced a rude awakening about the impact of prison on those who are incarcerated. I saw how much a man loses after being in jail for so long and how the system is set up for men, especially Black men, not to be fully equipped for re-entry into society after serving time.

After almost 20 years in prison, Juny was released with no trade, job preparation skills, or any assistance to get a job or find a place to live. His mother was still alive, so he had a place to stay. However, but I couldn't help but think about all of the people,

Juny in the federal prison on a visit with his wife and son Juice – 1994

who after being gone for that amount of time, literally had nowhere to go after being released. They would literally go from prison to homelessness. So, that helped me understand why so many people reoffend and go back to prison.

In a way, I can also say it has taught me something about society, the Black community, and the streets.

My cousin Juice's obituary – 2018

I also had another example of the negative outcome of choosing to live the street life. We tend to glorify the street hustler/gangster, but nobody talks about the aftermath. No one talks about the twenty-year prison terms, not being around to help raise your children, and not having anything left from that life except stories of when you were young and fly.

Juny is currently living in Denver, Colorado with his girlfriend, and he's still trying to get back on his feet financially. His only child, Lionel Reagor III, or Juice as the family called him, tragically died in 2018 from a gunshot wound to his chest. It was ruled an accidental self-inflicted shooting. The only witness was Juice's friend who claims Juice was playing around with his gun when it accidentally went off. He said he was pointing the barrel under his armpit as if placing it into a holster.

Juny does not believe that story. He believes that his son was murdered by his friend. Juny probably will not admit it, but you can tell Juice's death has taken a huge toll on him. I know, and I believe Juny knows, that Juice (along with me at one time), at the time of his death, was out here trying to live up to the PJ Fly persona we remembered and constantly heard about.

I'm sure it was even much easier for Juice to adopt that image as he was PJ Fly's son and namesake. This is only a guess, but I believe Juny feels somewhat responsible for Juice's death due to the example he set, not being around to raise him the right way. When he got out of prison, he did not make it clear to his only son that the street life was not the way to go.

QUAMÉ: When did you get the name Automatik and where did it come from (or who gave it to you)?

Rodney: The name Automatik came from my other uncle Artie, Juny's younger brother. Automatik was his street name. My father got a job in Houston, Texas, at the beginning of my ninth-grade year of high school. He moved the entire family pretty abruptly. I did not want to go but I was forced to. So, I planned to go to high school there and move back home to Los Angeles as soon as I was of age. I made no secret of those plans. Anyway, when I moved to Houston and started to get serious about rapping, I was going by the name G-Rod (Gangsta Rod). I was new to the school and also a freshman.

I met this 11th-grade dude named Jodrick or "J." J was super popular and looked the part. J was the representation of a real H-town street dude. He had the gold grill *way* before it was popular outside of Houston. He put me up on Houston swag. Jodrick took a liking to me and decided to take me under his wing. He was a rapper too. He asked me what my rap name was, and I told him G-Rod. He laughed and told me my name might have been a cool name in LA, but it was wack for Houston.

His rap name was Lil' Scooby because his uncle's street name was Big Scooby. He was always intrigued by my LA stories about my uncle and family in The Bottoms, so he said I should adopt my uncle's name. He did not think Lil Pimpin' Juny was a good Houston name either, so he asked me what my other uncle's name was and I told him "Automatik." He yelled, "That's it! That's your name! Young Automatik!"

I said, "Naw, that's not the uncle that I want to be like."

He said, "I don't care. That's a dope ass name and that's what I'm going to call you."

I tried to object and kept going by G-Rod, but he started calling me that in front of everybody, and since he knew everybody, it just stuck. When I made the freshman basketball team, everybody assumed the name had something to do with my jump shot being automatic. By that point, the name "Automatik" had a life of its own, so I just gave in and adopted it. Automatik it was! Later, when I started carrying pistols, people began to ask questions: "So is that where the name Automatik comes from because you always have an automatic pistol?" I said, "Okay, sure. That makes sense." That added to the allure of the name I guess.

Uncle Artie (Automatik) – 1982

QUAMÉ: What was your other uncle like, the uncle nicknamed Automatik? It's clear why you wanted to be like your uncle Juny,

but what was it about your uncle Artie that made you not want to be like him or take on his name? Is there something deeper there about your uncle Artie? What did he do for a living and what type of overall person was/is he?

Rodney: Uncle Artie is the youngest of Nonnie's five children. Because he was the baby of the family, he has always been kind of spoiled.

This caused him to have less drive than her other kids and to be more dependent on Nonnie for longer than the others. For most of my childhood, Artie was addicted to crack too. But Artie didn't smoke it out of a pipe like my parents. He was addicted to primos (crack mixed with weed, rolled in a joint). At the time, Artie was what they called "skanless," not scandalous, but "skanless." Skanless is worse than scandalous. People from LA know exactly what I mean. He used to steal money from my mother's purse and run off with people's money from the neighborhood all of the time. People would always come to Nonnie's house looking for Artie about something he had done. He was kind of the opposite of Juny.

Juny was a hustling go-getter that would give to the family not steal from it. The funny part about it is Artie was by far the smartest of Nonnie's kids. He is one of those people with a very likable personality and would keep you laughing for hours. He should've been a comedian, but he chose to use his intelligence and personality to try to get over on people, rather than make it beneficial to himself or the family. It got to the point where he started bragging about being the self-proclaimed "most skanless nigga in LA."

A funny fact about Artie is that he used to drive an ice cream truck through South LA when he was about 14 years old. He had long, permed hair that he would keep in hair rollers. It is rumored that he inspired the character "Big Worm" from the classic movie *Friday*.

He would tell us stories about how he would run off with people's money. His most used line was that he had a hook-up on guns because he knew all street dudes from LA always wanted guns. He would borrow someone's nice gun and use it as bait. Artie would entice them by saying he had the connections to get boxes of that gun. He would take them to the apartment building where my parents and I used to live because it had a secured front gate, but there was a back gate off of an alley. He would have somebody parked at the front of the building, and he would take the person's money to go and get the guns. Then he would go through the back gate to the alley where he would have somebody waiting in a car that he would leave in. He called this "back doe little joe."

When I was in the county, I met this dude who knew Artie. He told me Artie ran off with a few of his homeboys' money with the same gun story. I wasn't surprised at all. That was Artie in a nutshell. So that's why he wasn't the uncle I wanted to be like growing up. The irony to Artie's story and a testament to the glory of God is Artie is now very responsible and productive. He got off of drugs years ago, and is now the one who looks out for Nonnie the most out of her children. It's funny that the one that used to depend on her is now the one she can depend on most. For those reasons I tip my hat to him. He is an example of how God can deliver and redeem.

QUAMÉ: During one of our conversations, you said you had recently found out who *Rodney* was. How would you describe the "real" Rodney?

Rodney: Most people don't know the real Rodney. The real Rodney is an intellectual, spiritual, kind of shy kid who was extremely embarrassed that both of his parents were crack addicts. That was always a big secret (at least, I thought it was) to anybody outside of my family.

I constantly struggled to find my true self because stuff was always drastically changing as soon as I felt I was on a path to finding myself. For example, I was very good at basketball when I was a kid. I was making a name for myself in LA in the Little Leagues and AAU traveling teams. I was on a traveling team with Baron Davis and Paul Pierce, and it was a toss-up on who was the best player on the team between me and Baron. Anyway, just as I started ninth grade at Westchester High School (which was *the* basketball school at the time because they had just won the state title the year before, I believe) there was a drastic change. Everybody knew me at this school, and I thought, "Okay, this is what I'm supposed to do. I'm gonna play high school basketball good enough to at least get a college scholarship, get a degree, and maybe even go pro; you never know!" But two weeks later, after I impressed everybody and made the junior varsity squad, which was hard to do for a little man at Westchester by the way, my father up and moved us to Texas. I just had to adjust. However, I was an LA dude in Houston; I was different than everybody.

When I came back to LA, I had become kind of "country" because my formative years were in Texas, so I was still different, even back home.

QUAMÉ: Why do you think you were afraid to be Rodney instead of Automatik?

Rodney: I don't know if I was afraid to be Rodney. I think I just felt Auto was more interesting, more likable. Auto "pulled" every woman I ever had any type of relationship with, other than my ex-wife Nicole. She was the only girl attracted to Rodney, and I believe that had a lot to do with our relationship going on longer than it was supposed to.

I met Nicole on a school bus in Houston. I liked the fact that she was different from the other little, fast girls at school. She was quiet and, as I found out, the daughter of a pastor. She had and still has those morals instilled in her, which made her stand out from most girls where I was from. No one really knows this, but I always felt all of the other women liked Auto and what he brought to the table. Nicole loved the shy, fifteen-year-old kid, Rodney, before he had any money or even a car. Even though we grew apart, she always had that over everybody else.

QUAMÉ: Who is Yung Walt in relation to you, and how did your connection develop?

Rodney: Yung Walt is my first cousin. He is the son of my aunt Lanett, nicknamed "Piggy." Piggy is Nonnie's third born out of her five kids. Walt and I were very close. He was more like the little brother I never had because we lived with Piggy a lot when we were evicted due to my parents' crack addiction. I'd say we lived with Nonnie or Piggy for more than half of our time in LA before we moved to Houston. Also, when I moved back from Houston I moved in with Piggy. I was nineteen and Walt was around thirteen years old at the time. So, we both were glad to have the big brother/little brother thing back.

Back then, I took Walt everywhere with me, and I involved him in everything I was doing. I played basketball, so I took Walt to all of the courts with me. I rapped, so I took Walt with me to studio sessions and groomed him to start rapping. I wrote his early raps just to include him in what I had going. Walt had the charisma I didn't have. People liked him. That wasn't always the case with me, maybe because I was so quiet.

Since Walt and I did everything together. He had a bird's eye view of everything I was doing, even all of the mistakes. I tried to do my best to teach him the right way because his pops was not around much. However, I realize now that I wasn't the best role model at the time. I think he picked up some of my bad traits, and I regret that.

Somewhere along the way, our relationship strayed. I actually have no idea why. We didn't get into it or anything like that. Nonnie thinks when Walt got older he felt he needed to step out of my shadow. I don't know why that would be the case because it's not as if I was an NBA player or blew in rapping. So, in my opinion, he didn't have *big* shoes to fill, especially for there to be any resentment. But the truth of the matter is there *is* resentment for some reason. One day, I would really like to figure out where my relationship with my little brother went wrong. If it was something I did, I would like to know and possibly make amends for it.

QUAMÉ: How did your relationship with alcohol begin?

Rodney: When I was about sixteen years old, my father, who was an engineer, had been working in South America for a few weeks. When he returned, he brought some exotic tequila. For no apparent reason, one day, I decided to take some to school. I drank some at lunch. In my next class, which was the fifth period, I felt a little buzzed. One of the best-looking girls in the school was in this class. By nature, I'm a quiet, somewhat shy person, especially around gorgeous women, but that day I didn't care. I guess because I was buzzed. I was interacting with the class, the teacher, and most of all, that girl. She seemed to be feeling me. I'll never forget her saying to me, "We've been in this class for almost two months, and you never even spoke to me. I thought you didn't like me, but I see now that you are super cool."

From then on, we always spoke, hugged, and exchanged pleasantries whenever we saw each other. Nobody knew, but I was sure that being buzzed caused that. I felt it took away my natural shyness, made me relax, and even gave me the kind of confidence that was attractive to women.

QUAMÉ: What happened with the girl in class when you were buzzed? Did you two ever go out on a date? And how did you develop a pattern or routine of drinking?

Rodney: No, we never went out or anything. We were just really cool after that. We always spoke and hugged in the hallway and that was enough for me. It did wonders for my little confidence though. I never looked back in that area. In regard to drinking itself, I felt if I had a drink, it would give me the confidence to do what I did back in that classroom. So, whenever I was going out or in a social setting, I figured I would be a way better person if I had a drink.

QUAMÉ: Do you remember if there was any particular reason why you chose to drink that first time?

Rodney: There was really no particular reason I took that tequila to school. It wasn't a special day at school or anything like that. I just figured my lil' crew might want to check out the exotic tequila pops had brought back from South America.

CHAPTER 3

LOVE FOR BASKETBALL

Quamé: Rodney vs. Baron! What were some defining moments that solidified your ranking as one of the best at the time?

Rodney: Basketball was my very first love. I played it at the Inglewood YMCA since I was five years old. It came naturally. I became a prospect and one of the best in my age group at that time.

When I was twelve years old, a new dude entered the picture and people started asking if I had seen him play. I hadn't. But at that time, my confidence was so through the roof I immediately said, "He ain't better than me." After enough people said, "I don't know, Rod; this dude is good," I had to see for myself. So, I stayed after my game one Saturday to see what all of the fuss was about.

Me at the Inglewood YMCA Youth Basketball League – 1987

I watched Baron Davis demolish a pretty good point guard. At the time, I wouldn't admit it to anybody, but I knew he was really good, and a little bit of intimidation crept in.

Michigan was the favorite team to win the title that year. It was a stacked team with all of my friends from school on it. By the way, I was crushed when I wasn't picked to be on that team because another coach saw something in me and picked me to be on his team. Anyway, Michigan beat Baron's team pretty easily. The week before we were set to play Baron's team, we played Michigan. We were both undefeated. I had the game of my life. I scored thirty points, and we knocked off Michigan in double overtime with Baron watching. That basically solidified me as the best.

Well, the next week, our teams went at it. Everybody wanted to watch this game and to see Baron and me. The gym was packed. I was ready. I had confidence from the week before. Let's do it. Sidebar, the league had a rule. We played four, eight-minute quarters. To make sure every kid got a chance to play, during the first three quarters, the coaches had to take out the starters at the four-minute mark and put in the reserves.

To everybody's surprise, Baron's coach didn't start him. So, I went in and played against their starters but with their second-string point guard. I came out of the game with a three-point lead. Baron torched our second string and got them an eight-point lead. They did this for the entire first half. Baron and I didn't play against each other the whole first half. What I found out way later from Baron is that this was his coach's strategy. When they watched the Michigan game the week before, his coach felt we won because I played good defense on their point guard. He felt our second string was our weakness. It was working. At the half, we were down by ten points.

My coach didn't catch on to what they were doing. I had to literally tell him right before the second half started, "Coach, do you realize that Baron's coach is not starting him? He doesn't want him to go up against me." Baron's coach had six players looking like they were about to walk on the court. My coach had to yell out, "Coach, what five are you putting out on the floor?" He grinned knowing we had figured out his strategy, so he put his team out there without Baron.

I stayed out to wait for the second four minutes of the third quarter. Baron and I went at it. We both did our stuff. Even after having to climb out of a hole, my team came back. With ten seconds left in the game, we were down by only three. I took the last shot as the clock expired. I shot a three-pointer that would have tied it up and sent it to overtime. Clank! Off the side of the rim. Game over. Baron won.

The funny thing is the ref of that game happened to be the coach of an AAU traveling team sponsored by K-Swiss. He invited me to be on his team. A few weeks later, I went to the practice and who did I see when I walked into the gym? Baron. The ref had recruited him too. We both made the team, along with Paul Pierce who also played at the Y. The big talk was, "Who is going to be the starting point guard, Rodney or Baron? Well, we found out in the first game. Right when we were about to go onto the floor, the coach said, "Rodney, you got the point. Baron, you're at the two." I just smiled as I looked at everybody who realized what had just happened. He had won the head-to-head match-up game at the Y, but, at the end of the day, I started ahead of him on the AAU team. It always killed me to see him take off as he did and become a star in the NBA, and I didn't even get there.

The last time I saw Baron was at the end of the summer of my eighth-grade year and three weeks before we moved to Texas. I was walking down the street when a car pulled up and honked. It was Baron and one of the coaches of our AAU team. They asked where I was planning to go to high school, and I told them Westchester High School. As they were leaving, we told each other, "See you in high school," in a very competitive "can't wait to go at you" sort of way.

Weeks later, I was on the highway headed to Texas. The next time I saw Baron was on TV years later when he was the star of the UCLA Bruins. I always wondered what would've happened if I didn't move to Texas in my ninth-grade year. I thought, "My peers and the people I was compared to as kids are superstars in the NBA. They're not just in the NBA; they're stars. I should have at least made it there." Everything happens for a reason I guess. I played high school basketball in Texas, but it wasn't the same.

My parents' addition seemed to be worse in Texas, especially my mother. Before we moved to Houston, my father was always the bigger problem when it came to their addiction. Prior to moving, I had never seen my mother use drugs without my father there. She had never gone missing before or "on a mission" as my family called it unless it was with my father.

When we were evicted from our apartments, my mother and I would go and live with Nonnie, while my father and little sister would go and live with my father's mother. During those times, my mother would be clean the entire time we lived away from my father. In LA, my father did drugs with a lot of different people and went on missions a lot without my mother. Because of that, I always felt he was more of the problem. But when we moved to Houston, it flip-flopped.

In Houston, my mother became the one who would go missing for weeks at a time and do drugs with other people, but my father wouldn't. I believe being away from her family and comfort zone for the first time caused that problem. It probably took a huge toll on her just as much as it did me. It was chaotic in our home in Houston. My parents would have their addict friends living with us here and there, as well as running in and out of our place at all times of the night.

One day, I drove the car to school, which was rare because only seniors were supposed to drive to school. Plus, you had to pay for a parking pass. However, this one day, I was very hyped, and, after school, I pulled up to the front of the school to pick up my friends and to show off a little bit. My friends were talking to this other dude I knew. He said, "Auto, is that your car?"

I said, "Naw, that's my mom's car, but she lets me drive it," in the most humble-sounding way I could. As he was walking to the car he said, "This looks just like the dope fiend rental my older brother had the other day." A "dope fiend rental" is a car that an addict rents out to a drug dealer in exchange for drugs. When he got close to the car he said, "This *is* the same car because it has the same scratch on the passenger's door." He said that in front of all of my friends and some other people. At that point, I was extremely embarrassed. I tried to object by raising my voice and acting as if it would be a problem if he insisted, but I know the truth was written all over my face. The silence in the car afterward let me know I hadn't convinced anybody that it wasn't the dope fiend rental car.

Trying to keep my parents' household as normal as I could, looking after my little sister, and just being a kid with no support or structure caused me to miss a lot of school, which kept me off the basketball team at pivotal times in high school. I made the team and played my sophomore year and the first half of my junior year.

It wasn't my parents' fault alone that I didn't excel as I should have in my high school basketball career. I made some childish mistakes that I take full responsibility for. But I can say those experiences have helped me to be a better parent because I understand how important support and guidance are for a child during those formative years. I make it a point to put in extra effort during my daughters' formative years because I know it can make a big difference in their futures.

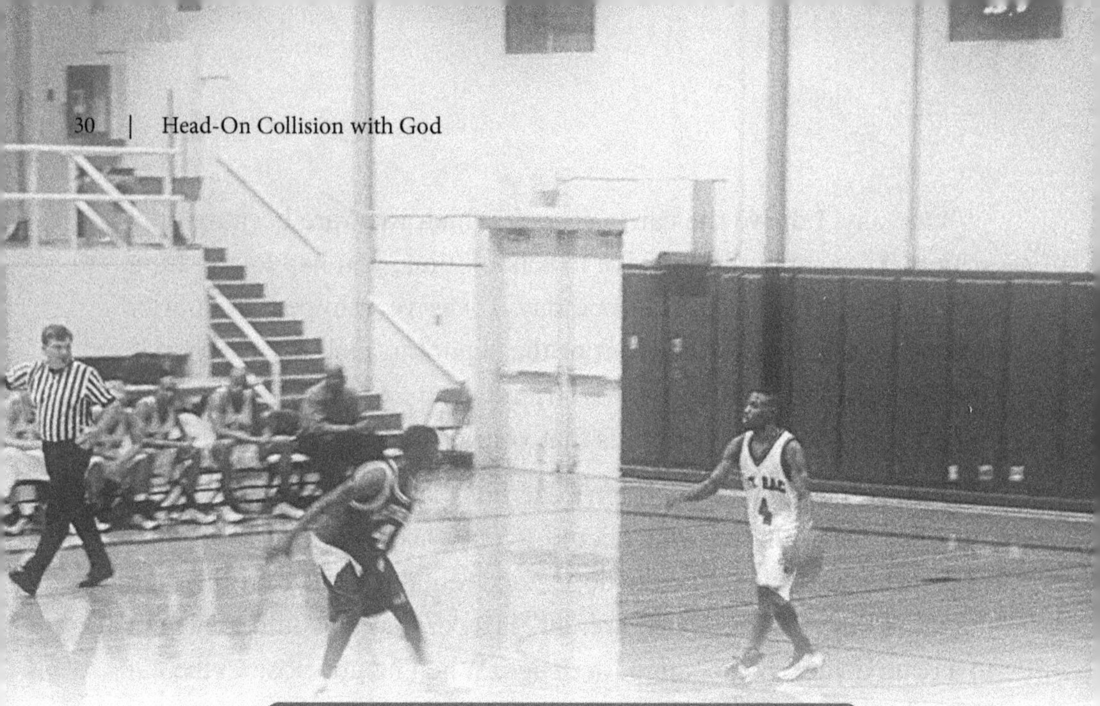

Me playing for Mt. San Antonio College – 1998

After high school, when I moved back to LA, I felt I wasn't given enough of an opportunity to play basketball in Houston, and my hoop dream wasn't over. I enrolled in Mt. San Antonio College or Mt. SAC and walked onto the basketball team.

MT SAC 1998-1999 MEN'S BASKETBALL

Rodney Wright **4**
5-10, 145, Freshman Guard Alief Elsik High School, TX

PRIOR TO MT. SAC
Averaged 12 PPG in High School...Dished out 7 assists per game...Career high of 27 points vs. Humble.

PERSONAL
Born May 23, 1978...Engineering major...Parents are George Wright III and Lanell Reagor...Rodney has a brother, George, and two sisters, Monica and Brianna...plans to become an engineer.

REDSHIRTS/GREYSHIRTS

These young men are part of the Men's Basketball Program at Mt. SAC. They are not participating this season, but their hard work in practice and support of their teammates will contribute to the team's success. The coaching staff is glad that they're here and looking forward to seeing them in uniform next year.

Dwain Gaines, *Chaffey College*

Gaven VanOver, *Serrano High School*

Mt SAC 28 Mounties

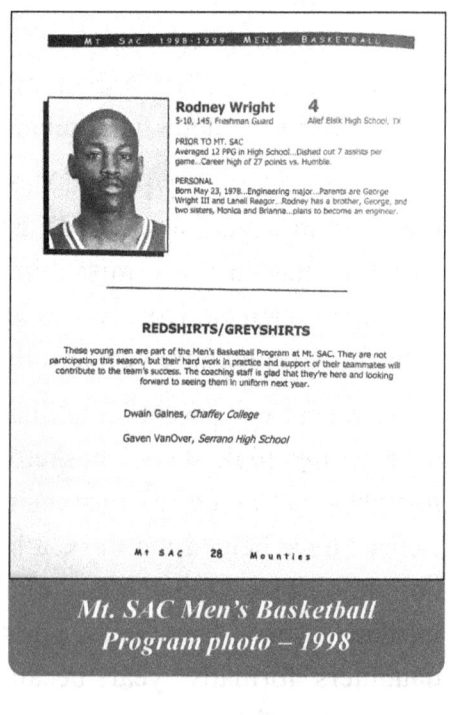

Mt. SAC Men's Basketball Program photo – 1998

I made the team and started for a while. At the time, I was living in LA and Mt. SAC was in Walnut, CA, which is about a forty-five-minute drive away. I had a run-down car that eventually broke down on me, which made it hard for me to get to school.

At the beginning of the following year, I applied for a job as a meter reader for the Southern California Gas Company and was hired. I had a baby girl with Nicole, who ended up joining me in LA. As a man, I had to take a stable job and drop out of school. I continued to play in adult basketball leagues throughout the city; that's how much I loved basketball. It was the only thing authentic to me. It doesn't matter what color or race you are, or where you come from, if you got game, you will be respected on the court.

About three years into working at the gas company, I was playing in this adult league in Compton. One night, there was a dude who was about 6'3" tall and was very good on the other team we were playing. It was a back-and-forth game. I had one of those games when I was "on" and killing the point guard on the opposing team. I scored forty points that night. In the third quarter, the 6'3" dude told his point guard he wanted to switch so that he could guard me. We went at it. I scorched him too.

After the game, I was walking toward the stands where Nicole was talking to a lady, who I found out was the 6'3" guy's wife. As we approached the stands, I heard her say to her husband, "Babe, he's good. You should get him on your team!" They came over to me and Nicole and said, "Hey, I play pro ball overseas. Are you interested in playing overseas? I'm sure I could get you on the team if you play anywhere near how you played tonight."

I took his number and called him. He was telling the truth. He showed me pictures and told me how they were treated like celebrities over there. It was in China or some other Asian country. He said all I needed to do was to get over there and he was sure he could get me a tryout and I would make the team. His proposition could've been my second chance. But I decided not to go. Nicole said that she would not go to China with me. Also, looking back, I have to admit I was somewhat intimidated about moving to a foreign country where I didn't speak the language. But most of all, I was scared of leaving my stable job and risking it all on what most considered just a "hoop dream." That decision still haunts me to this day. It's another one of those points in my life where I wonder "what if."

CHAPTER 4

AUTOMATIK THE MC

Quamé: When I met you in 2001, I only knew you as a top-tier MC. I honestly didn't know much else about you. I believed with all my heart you were going to be the next major MC to represent Los Angeles, along with your cousin Yung Walt. When and why did you first start rhyming? Do you still remember or have some of your very first lyrics?

Rodney: I was around ten years old when I first started rhyming. I was in the fifth grade and my teacher took our class on a field trip to a recording studio. My entire class recorded a rap song. We were all allowed two to four bars to rap, no hook. It ended up being like a five-minute song called the "Fifth-Grade Rappers." We all got a tape to take home to keep. Anyway, that's when I felt I could actually rap. Also, that was the time when Biv from New Edition came out with "Another Bad Creation," and shortly after, Kris Kross blew. At the time kid rappers were the fad. That's when it was born.

Quamé: What MCs did you listen to growing up or had the most influence on you?

Rodney: Super young, at the age of six or seven, I was a Run from Run-DMC head. Only to later figure out that DMC was the doper lyricist once I got into lyrics. But Ice Cube, Kurupt from the Dogg Pound, Pac, Nas, and Big were probably my biggest influences. To me, lyrically, Biggie had it though. Although, Pac was the best because of the emotions he brought out of people with his music.

Quamé: Are there any specific songs you feel impacted you in a significant way as a young Black kid?

Rodney: There are too many to name. I'm a real hip-hop head, so naming one song is a hard thing to do. I would say all of 2Pac's stuff around the time of the *Above the Rim* soundtrack, the *Me Against the World* album, all of the *Life After Death* Biggie album, "Dear Mama" by 2Pac, and oh, yeah, "Unbelievable" on Biggie's *Ready to Die* album.

Quamé: Can you give some specific examples of how those songs impacted you?

Rodney: "Dear Mama" by 2Pac impacted me a lot because I realized I wasn't the only person dealing with the emotions of having a mother on crack. I could relate to it on a whole other level. It's still very hard for me to listen to that song all the way through without

Me on stage rapping at a show – 2007

tearing up. And I have to say "Unbelievable" by Biggie because he was one of the most talented lyricists to ever touch a mic on a Primo track with the scratch hook. You can't get any better than that. It's the epitome of hip-hop at its finest to me. I patterned a lot of my style after my favorite artists. I wanted the wordplay like Biggie, with the feeling and emotions of Pac and the style and genuineness of Nas.

In my early 20s, when I realized the NBA dream wasn't panning out, I focused more on rap. I got a little bit of a reputation as a lyricist rapping with the Headbangaz, a crew of rappers and producers I linked up with where I used to get my haircut in the Crenshaw District. After that, I formed my own little crew, Skrilla Skwad, and started putting my own money into my rap career.

We started making some good music, and I was around a lot of talented artists who became big in the music industry. We did an album and a mixtape. I used my gas company and hustle money to get a professional video shot for the lead single on the album, *My Hood,* featuring and produced by Jason Edmonds of the iconic R&B group "After 7." We performed and did shows together. I even rented one of the most popular clubs in Hollywood at the time and booked a well-known act to open up for to promote the group. I paid for a commercial to run on 92.3 The Beat, a big radio station in LA, to promote the show and the group. None of these things came cheap at that time, by the way.

I got close to stardom but talent alone doesn't get you into the music industry. It got to the point where I had to decide on whether or not I was going to continue to pour money into my music career with no returns or invest my money in other things that seemed to have higher returns.

CHAPTER 5

HOME LIFE

Quamé: What's your relationship like with your child/children?

Rodney: Yes, I'm a father of four girls. My first two daughters, De'jah (23 years old) and Lyric (15) are by my ex-wife, Nicole, who was my high school sweetheart I met in Houston.

Nicole and I got married very young. I was about 23 years old. She was a nice girl, raised in the church, and the pastor's daughter. She was not promiscuous, and I liked that about her. I think we just grew apart, and our issues grew as I started to do better financially.

When my parents moved from Houston, I decided to stay there because Nicole had just given birth to De'jah. I wanted to be there with her and our child, so I stayed there at eighteen years old with no family and was still in high school. I had a little part-time job at a grocery store, and Nicole was working full-time so we thought we had enough to get a little apartment. Well, when my little bucket of a car broke down a month after my parents left, it got very difficult for me and my little family, and that put a gigantic strain on our relationship.

One day, after riding the bus to my grocery store job in the scorching Texas heat, my co-worker, who happened to be the boyfriend of one of Nicole's close friends, was picking up his check and about to leave. I asked, "Are you not working today?"

He said, "Naw, bro, I just quit. I can make more in one night selling dope than what we make here in a month."

A couple of months later, things got much worse for Nicole and me financially. It was so bad that her parents got involved. I overheard Nicole's mother say I was sorry and Nicole could do a lot better than me. Her parents refused to help us financially because we were not married and we were shacking up. This caused even more tension between Nicole and me. One day, we had a big argument and her mother came over. Nicole's mother said to Nicole, right in front of me, "You can do better than this. Look at Brandi. Her boyfriend just bought her a car and moved them into a townhouse."

I said, "Yeah, you know how he did it–he sells dope!"

Now, the next statement changed my perspective on life. I'll never forget these words from the pastor's wife as long as I live.

She said, "Well, at least he is handling his business as a man!"

That statement changed my life. At that point, I understood why Juny and others like him did immoral things and took penitentiary chances for money. It got them respect and admiration.

In my mind, if even the church people respected money over morals, then I was foolish for trying to do things the so-called right way. "Auto the Hustler" was born! Nicole and her mother stood by the front door of our apartment with their arms folded and told me I had to leave. I didn't have anywhere to go. I didn't have a car or any family for hundreds of miles. I ended up having to stay with a friend until my father was able to send me a bus ticket.

Me, Nicole, and De'jah – 1998

Fast forward about six years. I was promoted at the gas company, bought a condo, and was doing a lot better. A couple of years earlier, I was a part-time meter reader. That's when Nicole and I got married, mostly to get her parent's approval of our relationship. We did not have a wedding. We got married at a mid-week service in the church we attended at the time, owned by a pastor friend of Nicole's father.

But I never got over the mistreatment, being called "sorry," and kicked out of the apartment. I carried a chip on my shoulder. I realize now I hadn't completely forgiven Nicole for that treatment in Houston. When I started making money, I also started attracting more women, and it wasn't long before I was cheating on Nicole. It took me many struggles in my life for me to realize I was the reason for our divorce. I wasn't very mature or ready for a family.

Nicole moved back to Houston in 2008 with our two girls because of my escapades and arrogance. I cheated on Nicole with a woman named Cherisse, whom I had met during a marital separation. Years later, Cherisse became the mother of my third daughter, Kennedy (6 years old). I met Cherisse, a hairstylist, while she was working at the same barbershop where I met the rap crew the Headbangaz. She also seemed very different from the girls around the area.

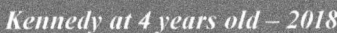
Kennedy at 4 years old – 2018

She was well-spoken and there was no hood in her. At that time, I was in full "Auto mode" and none of that impressed her at all. I had been trying to catch her eye for a while but to no avail. In fact, I had actually given up on her. One day, I entered the shop with my daughter De'jah in my gas company uniform. Cherisse told me later that she liked me from that point forward. She told me before that day that she thought I was just a young thug, rapper dude. However, she realized from seeing me with my daughter that I was a loving father and a working man. Also, her being five years older than me was different because she wasn't focused on the immature things that the women I was used to were focused on. Kennedy was conceived at a weird time in my life.

It was a transition time for me. I had just met the mother of my fourth daughter, who I will talk about soon. Cherisse and I were not together at the time, but I dipped back and slept with Cherisse one time just as my new

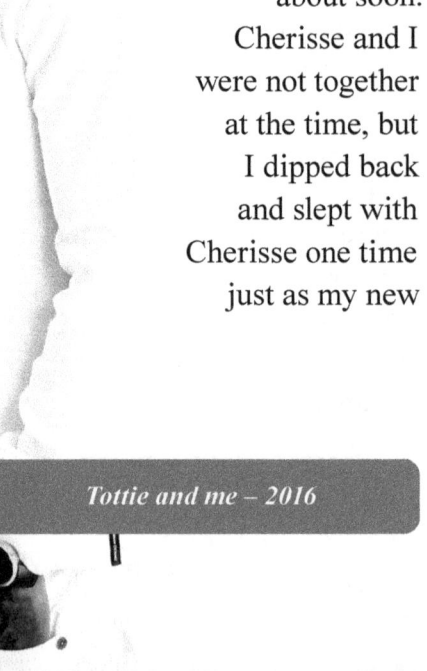

Tottie and me – 2016

relationship was starting. Kennedy was conceived. So technically, I cheated on Nicole and the mother of my fourth daughter with Cherisse. Cherisse is a very kind-hearted, supportive person. She is one of the nicest people I've ever met. She would give someone the shirt off of her back. But Cherisse was the only woman to ever cheat on me, which is the reason I didn't think we could ever be in a relationship, so I didn't want to have a child with her. My fourth daughter is Emory, (5 years old). Her mother's name is Totteanna or Tottie.

Tottie is the epitome of a ride-or-die woman. If she is with you, then you have a woman who has your back in any situation. If you are in a fight, she's throwing punches too. She is the most solid person, not just woman but *person,* I have ever met. The only downside to Tottie is that she is very stubborn and spoiled. So, when things don't go exactly her way, she can get mouthy and disrespectful. It reminds me a lot of how my mother used to talk to my father, so, of course, that was the *last* type of woman I wanted to be in a relationship with.

I met Tottie at a pool party in Las Vegas during Memorial Day weekend. The way it played out let me know that God really has a sense of humor. Anyone who has been to the festivities in Vegas during Memorial Dat weekend knows it is not somewhere you go to meet someone to have any type of serious relationship. As a matter of fact, I remember this statement that everybody was posting on social media that weekend, "If any man in LA is looking for a wife this weekend, now is the time because all of the hoes are in Vegas!" And I was absolutely fine with that, because the last thing I was looking for that weekend was a wife.

The way I met Tottie was definitely orchestrated by God. I was walking through the lobby of the hotel and casino and I saw a group of about six good looking women. I turned to my cousin to ask him did he see what I saw. To my surprise he was gone. I was shocked because he was just there a split second before. It was like he vanished in thin air. I realize now that was also orchestrated by God because he was already pretty tipsy and may have ruined the initial meeting.

Not wanting to let this group pass me by I said something to them to let them know that I was interested. About four of them turned around all inquiring trying to figure out which one of them I was talking about. Sidebar: Any man who is at all seasoned at approaching a group of women already knows that the last thing you should do is start the conversation by choosing a particular one because if that one is not interested then the others will not give you the time of day because they would not want to be your back up choice. Well as they were asking me which one of them I made the comment to, something in my head as clear as day said, "THAT'S HER!" And before I was able to stop myself I said, "I'm talking to you", as I pointed to Tottie. Immediately I snapped out of it and said to myself, "Why did you just do that?" But it was too late. She was headed my way. The rest is history.

What God later revealed to me is that He ordained that meeting. He wasn't going to let me, my cousin, or anybody else ruin the meeting that He orchestrated that day. What I didn't know was that years before God had trained this woman to be able to deal with the life changing situation that I would go through years later. When Tottie was about 20 years old, the first man in her life, her father, was arrested and went through the same court system that I would eventually have to go through. She had to learn how to provide for herself after her primary breadwinner was abruptly removed from her life. She was forced to deal with lawyers, jail visits, and court dates at an early age. By the way, her father and I have the same birthday if you needed anymore confirmations. God told me that He loves me so much that He wasn't going to let me block my own blessing by saying something stupid. God had already trained this woman to be what I needed before I knew that I was going to need it. My plan was to go to Vegas, have some fun, and get back to my unfulfilled life. But God had other plans.

As I stated, Cherisse is a nice girl, but I didn't think we could be in a relationship, so I didn't want to have a child with her. Emory's mother was new, and kind of volatile at times, so I didn't want to have kids with her either. When these two girls came, I was confused and somewhat upset with myself. Emory was born in August of 2016, and my accident was in January 2017. At the time, I was very lost and confused. I never thought of myself as one of those dudes who would have four kids by three different women. And at the time, I didn't think that I would be with any of the mothers, which hurt me even more. I was lost. I tried to mask my hurt by going out and drinking with associates several times a week.

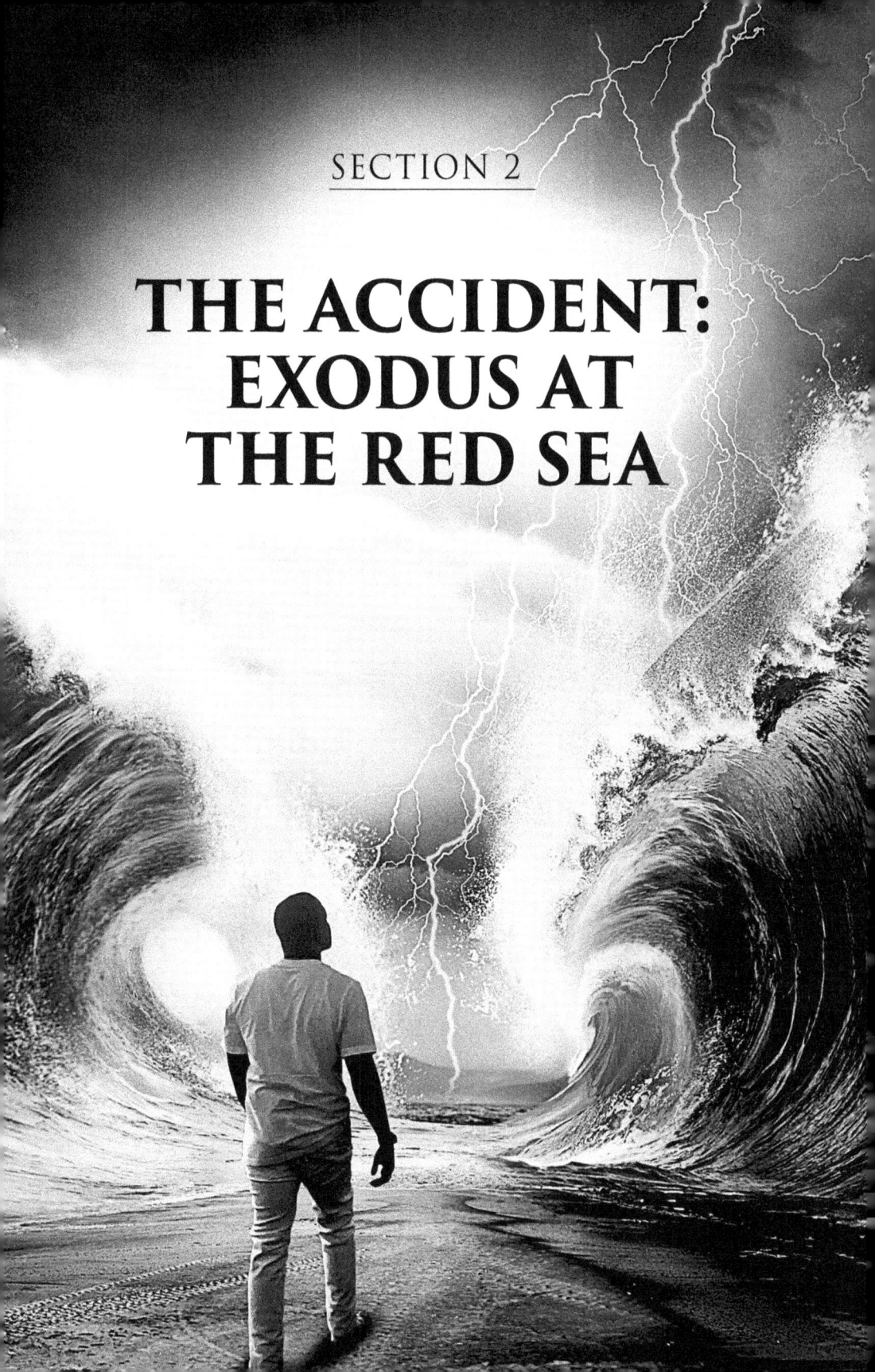

CHAPTER 6

THE SPIRAL

Quamé: What happened that evening before the accident occurred? What were you doing and why? Describe in detail the events leading up to the actual accident.

Rodney: The accident itself was early in the morning of January 21, 2017. Let's back up to 2016, so I can give you the backstory. During the second half of 2016, things really came to a head with me. I was in a somewhat new relationship with Tottie. Emory, my youngest daughter, was born to us on August 3, 2016.

Tottie and I bought a house and moved in early May 2016 while she was still pregnant. Cherisse and I were not together at the time, but our relationship did overlap with the relationship I had

Emory at one year old – 2017

with Tottie. Kennedy, my daughter with Cherisse, was about two years old at that time, and Emory was about to be born. Because of that overlapping period, amongst other things, Cherisse was still holding on to the idea of us possibly getting back together. Nicole was also holding on to the same idea, and I didn't know that at the time. Nicole had no idea that Cherisse (the woman I had cheated on her with back in 2008) and I had reconnected. Additionally, neither Nicole nor our two daughters knew Cherisse and I had a daughter, Kennedy. By the way, they also didn't know about my new relationship with Tottie, that we had a house, and she was pregnant.

My whole life at that point was chaotic and wrapped up in deceit and secrecy. I see now the way I was navigating the situations and interacting (the little things that I was saying and doing) with these women is why they were holding on to the possibility of relationships with me. However, back then, I didn't understand my ways or the effect I had on these women. When I moved into my home with Tottie, most of the people closest to me didn't know that I was in a serious relationship.

Nicole and my two children thought I was living in LA, single. Nicole hoped that we would get married if I "got my stuff together". To rationalize the dishonesty in my mind, I looked at it this way, "Why should I tell Nicole and my kids about Tottie when I'm not even sure I'm going to be with her due to her volatile side that I was just finding out about." Regardless, I was moving *way* too fast! But as it always does, it all hits the fan.

Somehow, Nicole found out about my new girl Tottie and the house we had just bought. She must have thought, "Wow, he must really like this girl because they bought a house together. They're serious and that means we're definitely not getting back together!" But when it happened, I had to break the news to my oldest daughter, De'jah, who was attending Baylor at the time. I flew out to Houston to break the news to her in person. It was devastating to my daughters and especially to my ex-wife.

After that, Nicole attacked me in every way she could. She went to child support services. I received paperwork saying she had filed a complaint stating that I hadn't contributed *any* money to the raising of my children since our divorce nine years prior.

I could not believe it because every two weeks, when I got paid, I would send her money. I was also paying for most of De'jah's college tuition, and I had bought her a brand-new car. Everything she asked for, I gave. So, it really hurt me when she lied just to spite me (in my mind). Child Support demanded I pay $54,000 by the next week and if not, they threatened to garnish my wages. This happened in September 2016.

What made things even worse was when I found out how Nicole learned about Tottie. Somebody in my family told her I had a new girl and it seemed kind of serious. Nicole went through my social media and found Tottie's page somehow. Then Nicole contacted Tottie via social media. She messaged her and said that she was my ex-wife and so on. Tottie confirmed what Nicole had heard. I received a text message from my ex-wife going off on me about how I was spending all of my money on another women and her child. When I got home, I asked Tottie what was going on and where Nicole got that information from. Tottie told me that Nicole had messaged her, and she went off on Tottie. I asked to see her phone and she showed me the messages. It was a very touchy conversation to say the least.

From that point on, I was pissed at everybody. I was pissed that my ex, who I've known since I was fifteen years old, would lie and discredit me as a father. I totally understood Nicole saying I was a horrible husband, but I didn't understand her discrediting me as a great father and provider to my children. I was kinda upset at Tottie because, at the time, I felt she could have held her composure in that situation, instead of somewhat fueling the fire. But I now realize that would've been a difficult task for anybody. I was also pissed at my family member for telling Nicole in the first place. I was always taught, right or wrong, you should never side against your family. But above all I was mad at myself for letting the situation spiral out of control and letting my dishonesty compound like I did.

As the summer was ending, I was being attacked left and right. I received paperwork every other day that talked about garnishing wages and court dates. I had to hire an attorney and fight against the lie that I was not supporting my children. I'd been supporting my children since I was eighteen years old. I was honorable when it came to supporting my children. However, the courts seemed indifferent to what I was saying and said I had to prove it!

All of that drove a wedge between the relationships I had with Tottie and my children. My children were hearing all these crazy things, and they didn't know what to believe. All of this put me in a dark place at that time because I never wanted to be a "baby mama" type of dude. That's why I married my ex-wife when my daughters were young. I said to myself I wasn't going to be the kind of guy with baby mamas everywhere, but lo and behold, there I was.

I went from having a wife with two daughters a few years ago to having four daughters by three different women in a two-year period. And to make matters worse, due to the situation that occurred between Tottie and my ex-wife, I started to question my relationship with Tottie. I figured I wasn't going to be with Emory's mother either. However, I had to contend with how I would get out of the situation since I had just bought a house with Tottie, and we had a newborn. I was confused, drained, and depressed. I felt I had made a big mistake.

I would pray and ask God, "God, if this Tottie girl is not "*the* one", why would you allow all of this to happen?"

There was a court date in December 2016 that Nicole and my daughters had to fly out for. I was sitting in the waiting room at the courthouse when they walked in. I hadn't seen my daughters in about six months at that time. When they walked in, they all looked at me, turned, and walked off to the other side of the waiting room without saying anything. That moment confirmed my daughters were upset with me and on their mother's side. I was the bad guy. They didn't say a word, wave, or anything. That hurt. To have my children against me when the truth was I had been providing for them the entire time hurt beyond belief. They knew I had been taking care of them financially, but we were there basically because of a woman's scorn. She lied and said I had never taken care of my daughters. Ironically, they were at the courthouse wearing the clothes I had probably bought them; yet, they weren't even speaking to me. That happened a few weeks before the accident and it bothered me.

All of that stuff, what I did, and the position I put myself in had my whole life up in the air. So, during that time, I just threw myself into work. I was working like crazy. In my mind, the situation was about money, so I started working around the clock taking double shifts.

My depression had gotten so bad that I could no longer get proper sleep. On some workdays, I had to be at work by 7:00 a.m., so I would wake up at 5:00 a.m. When I got home to go to bed by about 10:00 p.m., I couldn't go to sleep. I had insomnia. It would be 3:00 a.m. and I still couldn't fall asleep. I would be extremely tired, but my mind would be racing with thoughts. So, by the time 4:00 a.m. hit, I would not bother to even try sleeping since I would have to be up in an hour or so anyway. I would go back to work and do a twelve to fourteen-hour workday with no sleep. This wasn't every night, but it happened enough that it was taking its toll.

It wasn't until months later that I learned depression can cause insomnia. Anyway, one of my friends at the time gave me a Xanax pill and said to take a quarter of it when I couldn't fall asleep. He told me, "Bro, these knock you out, like *out* out." You know when somebody says a word twice to describe something the person really means it. He gave me a couple and said, "Don't ever take a whole one; just cut it and take a quarter." I did what he said, and he was right. It was the best sleep I had in my entire life!

During that time, I had been going out a lot more. I didn't want to be home because I was having second thoughts about Tottie. I was going to clubs, lounges, day parties, pool parties, strip clubs, whatever. I was out.

I was hanging out with people who weren't working a job like me. They didn't have to wake up early like me, so they had a different relationship with time. Getting home at 2:30 a.m. was nothing for them, but it was a huge issue for me because I had to be up by 5:00 a.m. I didn't want to be at home to face the reality I created, so it didn't matter. I felt, "I'll just go home basically to shower and sleep." Of course, my absence from home was causing even more issues between Tottie and I.

My life was chaotic. Every day I asked, "What am I going to do? God, why would you allow all of this to happen? I have problems in my house." There was also chaos with my other daughters. All of this was affecting my quality of life, so the only thing I could do was what I later learned a lot of people do when life is piling up on them—self-medicate.

CHAPTER 7

THE COLLISION

Here is something very important that most people didn't know at the time of my accident. At the beginning of every year, for the last fifteen years, I fast to start the year off. Starting the second Sunday of January for twenty-one days, I fast. I don't eat any meat or watch television, and I only ingest things grown from the earth, the "Daniel Fast" is what it is called.

My father and I have Lakers season tickets. We try to sell every set of tickets except the games we want to go to. The only time we might consider going to a less desirable game is when those tickets don't sell. The website releases the tickets back to us as unsold maybe two hours before the game tip-off. So, on Friday, January 20, 2017, my father called me at about 5:30 p.m. and informed me that our Lakers tickets did not sell. He asked if I wanted to go or just let the tickets go to waste. Normally, during my fasting period, I don't engage in any activities like that; everything is off–no parties, no television, no soda, nothing. But that year, with depression and all of the horrible things going on in my life with the court situation, Nicole and my children, Kennedy and Cherisse, and my failing relationship with Tottie and my new daughter Emory, I felt like I could amend my fast.

In hindsight, I now see I was mad at God for allowing me to go through what I did, and I felt entitled to break the fast. Most of the people around me never went to church, paid tithes, or ever fasted, and they seemed to be prospering. They definitely weren't depressed. They weren't being attacked as I was. They did whatever they wanted and their lives seemed to be *way* better than mine. "So why do I always have to be the godly example?" I asked myself. "There is obviously no benefit in being that way because if there is, He [God] would not allow my ex-wife, who was clearly lying on me, to be winning." So, I broke my fast for the first time ever and decided to go to the game. No big deal, right? Later, I was told of a Scripture verse that let me know just how big of a mistake that was.

> When you make a vow to God, do not delay to fulfill it. He has no pleasure in fools; fulfill your vow. It is better not to make a vow than to make one and not fulfill it. (Ecclesiastes 5:4-5 NIV)

I later realized my declaration to God that I would fast was a vow and breaking the fast was breaking a vow to God. That is serious. But I was arrogant, lost, and in my feelings toward God at the time. And besides, I was just going to a basketball game; that's not a sin.

I went forward with my efforts, but I had a few hiccups I later realized were my warnings and potentially my way out of what was to come. I asked my father if he was going with me to the game. If my father had gone, most likely, I would have ridden with him to the game, gone straight home, and gotten to sleep at a decent time so I could get up to go to work the next morning. He said he couldn't go. I called one of my responsible friends and invited him to go. He said he couldn't go. Those were two opportunities for me to avoid trouble that evening. However, I persisted. I called my "turn-up" friend, Roy. You know that friend who is always down to go out. Of course, he said, "Yes," as I knew he would. As I was getting dressed, Tottie said to me, "Don't go out or to the sports bar after the game because you know you have to go to work in the morning (a warning)."

"I'm not going anywhere after the game," I explained to Tottie sternly. I had no plans of doing so.

In 2 Samuel, King David committed his greatest sin, adultery. As a result, he murdered one of his loyal soldiers because he wanted his wife. The punishment for this sin was costly and changed David's lineage. I was familiar with this story already. What I didn't realize was a very important, yet, small detail pointed out at the beginning of the story:

> It happened in the spring of the year, at the time
> when kings go out to battle... but David remained in
> Jerusalem. (2 Samuel 11:1)

David's first mistake was that he wasn't where he was supposed to be. He was supposed to be on the battlefield. That was also my first mistake. I wasn't where I was supposed to be: at home fasting, not at a basketball game. Those first small mistakes, if ignored, can lead to giant sins that can change your life as you know it. Also, in verse three it says:

> So David sent and inquired about the woman, and
> someone said, "Is this not Bathsheba, the daughter
> of Eliam, the wife of Uriah the Hittite?
> (2 Samuel 11:3)

David was informed of exactly who the woman was and that she was married, but he persisted. He had his warnings and ways out just as I did, but we did not take heed.

While Roy and I were at the game, we started getting calls from some friends who said, "Hey man, we're at the GS Sports Bar, come through!" I went, but I wasn't supposed to be at a place like that during my fast. I wasn't supposed to be at the game either, so I decided to roll. When we got there, as usual, they were buying rounds of Vodka and Hennessy. I said, "Nah, I'm good." Eventually, I had some wine. Typically, I don't even drink sodas or anything other than water or 100 percent fruit juice during my fast. Any type of alcohol is *way* out of the question, but the voice in my head whispered, "It's just wine. Jesus and His disciples drank wine. Wine is from grapes so technically..."

I had to be at work for overtime the next morning, which was Saturday, but I stayed at the sports bar until it closed at 2:00 a.m. I had to be up by 5:00 a.m. for overtime, which was mandatory because I had requested it. This night had really snowballed into something I never intended it to be. So, I pulled out of the parking lot to head home.

This is usually a straight shot home, north on the 405 Freeway most of the way. Somehow, at some point, I ended up going in the wrong direction on the 405 Freeway. This caused a horrible head on collision that took the lives of two young men, brothers, and left me

Freeway picture of my smashed truck

in critical condition clinging to life. I had (and this was confirmed by Roy and everyone at the sports bar) about three or four glasses of wine and then I left. Witnesses say I was going southbound on the northbound side of the freeway doing approximately 65 mph. I was going the wrong way on the freeway at a high speed and the other car was traveling at a freeway speed also.

I always wear my seatbelt, but the first responders and the police report stated I was found in the backseat of my car. How could that be? There is no logical way I could have been driving at that speed with a seatbelt on and end up lying in the backseat after a head-on collision. Also, the front end and the engine of my truck were pushed into the front seat due to the force of the collision. Anything in the front seat of my truck should have surely been crushed. The Word says:

> The angel of the Lord encamps around those who
> fear [reverence] him, and he delivers them.
> (Psalm 34:7 NIV emphasis added)

I envision just as that collision was about to take place, an angel shielded me from being crushed and placed me in the backseat or allowed me to get in the backseat even with all of my injuries. Even if you are not a believer, you have to admit that was a miracle!

I think about that miracle very often. I wonder why God "saved" me or left me here. I put the word "saved" in quotation marks because the world says I was lucky to be saved or spared. The world believes being left here on the earth was a good thing. But what does the Word say?

> To be absent from the body is to be present with
> the Lord. (2 Corinthians 5:8)

Jesus told the repentant criminal next to Him on the cross:

Today, you will be with Me in paradise. (Luke 23:43)

Maybe God showed the two young men He took home that evening favor and took them from here early as a reward. Perhaps I was left here as a punishment. Or maybe I have more work to do for Him. I've watched a lot of interviews and listened to people who have had brief afterlife experiences where they technically died but came back. Most of them have said it was very peaceful and an amazing experience. One guy said he was extremely upset when he woke up in the hospital and realized he was back on the earth after experiencing that kind of peace.

What I know is this world is not a peaceful place. It's full of wrath, violence, vengeance, and a complete lack of compassion. It doesn't sound anything like paradise. The world has a saying, "The good die young," and the more I hear about those young men, the more I find out about how good they were. Maybe an early pass to paradise together was the way God honored their goodness.

CHAPTER 8

MY INJURIES

I made it out of the accident alive, but just barely. I sustained multiple injuries:

- » Broken right foot
- » Broken left tibia – came through the skin
- » Compound fracture
- » Broken ribs
- » Head trauma requiring two brain surgeries
- » Broken thumb
- » Broken hand
- » Broken neck
- » Centimeters from being paralyzed from the neck down
- » In a coma for a while, unresponsive on arrival at the hospital

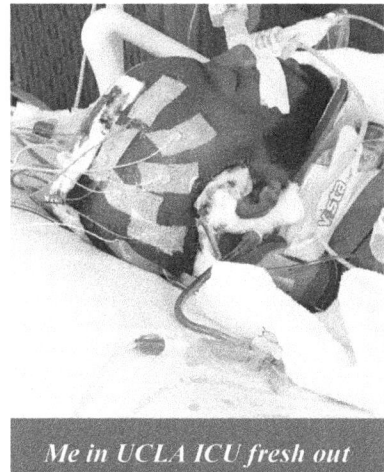

Me in UCLA ICU fresh out of surgery – January 21, 2017

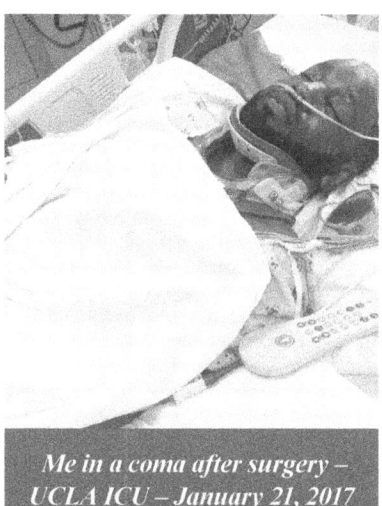

Me in a coma after surgery – UCLA ICU – January 21, 2017

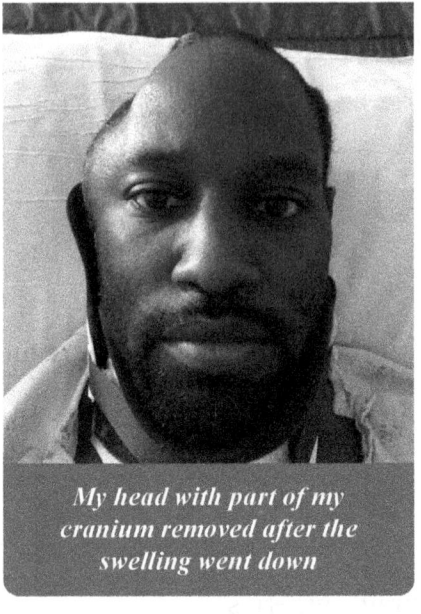

My head with part of my cranium removed after the swelling went down

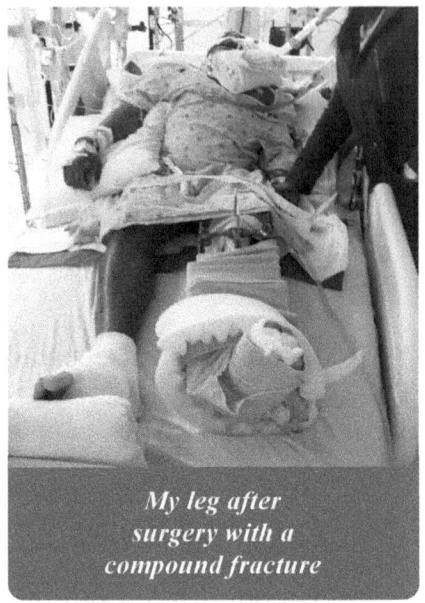

My leg after surgery with a compound fracture

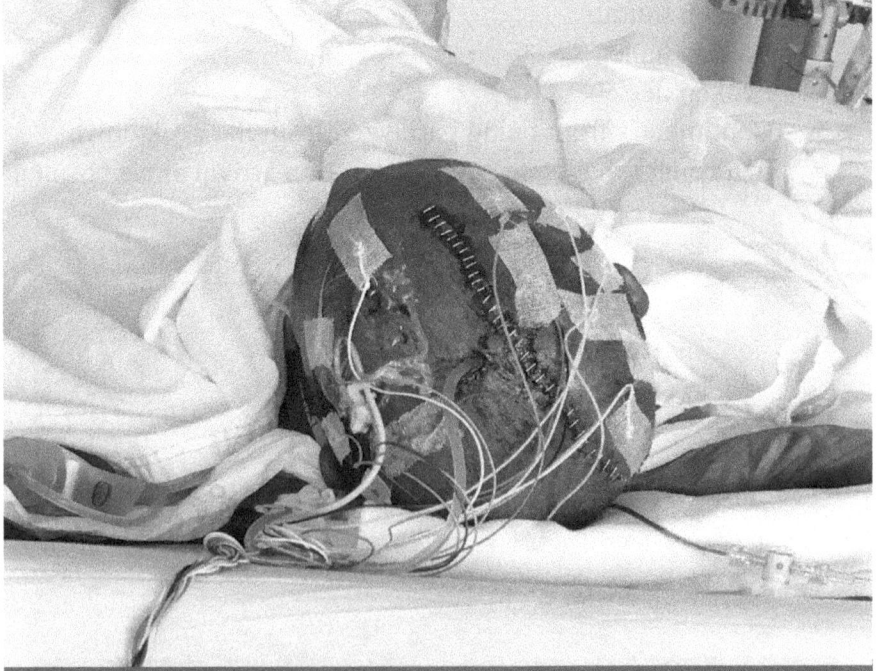

Blood being drained from my head while in a coma

Quamé: You woke up in the hospital. Were you handcuffed?

Rodney: By the grace of God, I wasn't handcuffed. Nobody told me anyone other than myself had gotten hurt in the accident. My father decided not to tell me the entire situation at first because the doctors told my family due to the severity of my injuries, I would have to really want to live to pull through. My father felt if I knew the whole story I may not have wanted to live, and he was right. I think he made the right decision. From what I hear, it was touch and go. If I knew what I had to endure if I recovered, I probably would have given up. Fighting to have a normal life is hard enough. I may not have considered it to be worth it to fight for a life that may turn out to be hell.

Tottie and my sister Monica took turns spending the night with me in my hospital room. I don't remember much about the hospital but I do remember when they were there and because of that I did not feel alone. They probably don't know this but they motivated me to fight harder and to want to recover. Every time I take a step it is a testament to them and I will always remember who was in the hospital with me when I couldn't take a step.

The detectives came to talk to me, but I was so out of it due to the brain surgery and medication, I don't remember much of anything they said. My family told me the police came because there was damage on the freeway, property damage, and the city may seize my personal assets. Also, the detectives didn't have the toxicology reports yet, so they were just gathering information. The investigators were pursuing a case, but the entire time, I didn't know people had died. My family told me because of the property damage and a possible DUI, I should retain a lawyer. I did.

Before the detectives came to the hospital, the police had returned my backpack that they found at the accident to Tottie. When I came to and was able to talk and think straight, Tottie informed me she had gone through my bag and found a piece of one of my Xanax pills. She asked me if I had taken a piece of one of the pills that night. I said it was possible, but I couldn't remember. I couldn't remember anything from that night at the time. What I could remember is I had recently gotten those pills and didn't need to take any, so there was no reason for a piece to be missing. When Tottie told me about the pill, I was nervous that I had probably taken a piece of the pill that night but also anticipated what the toxicology reports would say.

I had already secured a lawyer and when they finally told me about the lives lost, I was out of the hospital and in a rehabilitation home learning how to walk again. I was in the hospital for about four months, including the time at a rehabilitation home. The four months seemed long because I had a broken leg, broken foot, and broken neck. I had to wear a neck brace 24 hours a day, which made it very difficult to sleep.

After getting a little better in the rehabilitation home, I walked about four or five steps from the bed to the door by myself.

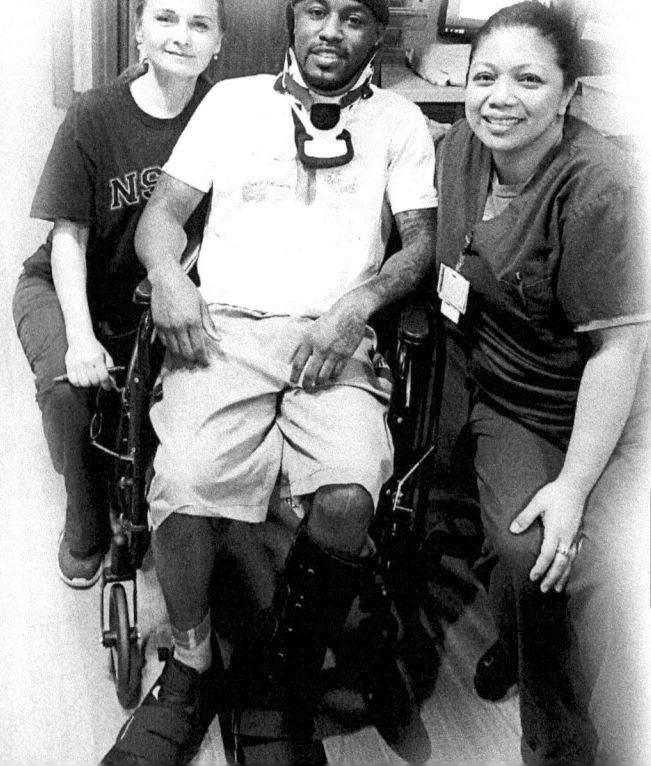

My physical therapist, nurse, and me in the rehabilitation home

The nurses and physical therapists cheered "Yaaaaaaaaay!" That's how bad my injuries were. Walking five feet was a great accomplishment. I think back now on those moments and I feel so grateful to God all over again because I realize how far I've come. Being able to stand up and take showers without my walker was my next big accomplishment. I was happy to see my body actually becoming somewhat normal again.

It was a slow, grueling process, but it was happening. It was like starting over again, literally. I couldn't walk without using a walker. However, I rolled in there in a wheelchair not knowing when or even if I would walk the same again. I went from not walking, to walking with a walker to the bathroom, to walking five feet without the walker, to walking to the front door of the rehabilitation home, to walking half of a block. All of this with the help of an amazing physical therapist. She was the biggest help to me being able to walk again. She was also one of those people who had very interesting stories, and we used to talk for hours, which came in handy at that time because I had just found out people had died in the accident. Walking and talking with her took my mind off what was to come.

Regarding jail, my lawyer said I was not a flight risk and he had already contacted the authorities. Since they knew where I was, we were waiting for them to call and let him know when they were ready to start the criminal proceedings. My lawyer said most likely, they would charge me with vehicular manslaughter. He said he would accompany me when I turned myself in, and then I would be able to post bail. He also said we were going to fight it and hopefully get a deal for a lesser charge because I didn't have a record. But it didn't go like that at all.

CHAPTER 9

THE ARREST

Quamé: What was the process like when you were first arrested?

Rodney: The arrest process was scary. It was unexpected and I believe very unnecessary. I got out of the rehabilitation home, and I was still going to the hospital to get occupational and physical therapy. The day I was arrested, I was going home from the hospital. The doctor had just told me he would give me six more weeks off from work because my left leg still had a slight fracture. When I left the hospital, on the way home, the police swooped on me like SWAT. It was crazy! They had about eight cars and hopped out with automatic rifles aimed at me! They yelled, "Don't move! Where are the guns?" I was very confused and thought to myself, "This can't be for me. Maybe there was a robbery in the area today and this car fits the description." But they kept yelling, "Where are the guns?" Finally, one of them said, "Are you Mr. Wright?" I said to myself, "Yeah, this is for me."

They snatched me out of the car and handcuffed me.

I found out later they were yelling about guns because they knew I had three guns registered to me. Then I heard the officer say something I will never forget: "Yeah, we have the 187 suspect in custody." When he said that, I thought to myself that he must have made a mistake. I said, "Excuse me; what do you mean 187?" The officer said, "Yeah, you're charged with two counts of murder." When he said that an indescribable feeling went through my body. It was one of despair mixed with horror and shame all at the same time. My heart just sank. I said, "Are you sure about that because it was a car accident; this is vehicular manslaughter."

At that point, the officer held up some paperwork and said, "Man, do you see this?" When I looked at the paperwork, sure enough, it said two counts of 187. The officers came to arrest me for murder, not vehicular manslaughter. They treated me as if I had shot and killed people. They didn't even know there was a car accident. When they sent that tactical force, they just told them to get me for murder and I was armed and dangerous. They did not know the guns they were talking about were simply my personal guns registered in my name. Later, this part made me understand the Breonna Taylor shooting a lot more.

As I was talking to the officer, I noticed a shift in how he was treating me as he went through my wallet and saw my work identification card. He asked, "So how long have you worked for the gas company?"

I said, "Since I was nineteen years old. This is not what they presented the situation to be. I had a car accident."

Then the officer said, "Oh, okay, yeah, they do that sometimes."

From that point, they were kind of chill with me. They even met with Tottie to let her get my bag, car keys, and my wallet. Initially, they came to capture a murderer and their mindset was, "We will kill him out here if he makes a false move." Imagine going from what my lawyer told me about turning myself in to the situation I just described. Nonetheless, I was very glad I wasn't at home because they would have kicked my door in, involved my neighbors, and my family would have been at risk.

SECTION 3

PRISON

THE WILDERNESS

CHAPTER 10

PROCESSING

After the arrest, the next part was processing. These were actually the worst three days of my life–by *far*! It was worse than the worst days of my childhood. It was worse than even my near-death injuries. It was worse than the time in the county jail and the time in prison. It's horrible how they treat people. I was probably at about 60 – 65 percent physical ability. The doctor had just told me my tibia was still broken. I had just gotten to the point where I was working out the rest of my body, and I was walking without using a walker, but I was nowhere near normal.

LA Men's Central Jail (The County Jail)
Downtown Los Angeles

I spent three days in the processing area of the county jail. That's where they figure out where they're going to house you. You're basically in a big tank with a bunch of other guys. Imagine hundreds of people crammed in a room. It's very cold and there's nothing in there but the floor and a few steel benches. They bring you a peanut butter and jelly sandwich every six or seven hours or so. I couldn't believe all my tax money went to that. It's worst than how animals get treated. And I had to endure those conditions for three whole days, seventy-two hours–no shower, no real food, no real place to sleep.

I was just coming off of major surgeries. I had a big scar on my head from my second brain surgery, and no one cared even a little bit. I would lay on the floor trying to sleep, but you really can't get sleep in a situation like that. The only clothes I had were some basketball shorts and a small T-shirt. They take away your shoestrings and anything they feel you can use to harm somebody. It was freezing. I was in there with hundreds of people, all pissed because they were in jail. Fights were happening all the time. It was the worst part of this whole thing, being treated like an animal. They herd people in there like cattle.

Finally, after three days, I got housed. Now, I've never been through the county jail process before. Although I had been to jail before, it was just overnight in a holding station, but being transferred downtown to the county jail was an entirely new situation. The couple of times I was arrested previously, I bailed out at the holding station well before I would be transferred to the county jail. So, all of this was new to me.

CHAPTER 11

LIFE IN THE THUNDERDOME - 2400 BLOCK

I finally got housed. About twelve of us were walking down a long hallway handcuffed to each other. Then the officer started telling people where they would be housed. He said, "You seven, you're going to 2400, and you two are going to 5400," and so on.

I didn't know what any of that meant, but I was part of the seven who were going to 2400. At that point, this one dude started yelling, "Ah, yeah, it's going down, Thunderdome! Y'all better be ready to squabble or roll it up! We're headed to the Thunderdome where it goes down!"

"Oh, my God, is this really where I'm going?" I thought. A couple of people I was talking to in processing said I would probably go to a medical dorm because of my injuries. There was no way they would send me to regular housing. But for some reason, that didn't turn out to be the case. As guys around me were getting hyped up about going to the Thunderdome, I got anxious. God seemed to have turned His back on me and life kept getting worse. For some reason, God was putting me through hell. Maybe He was upset with me because of the accident and the death of those two young men that evening. This was one of the darkest moments of my entire life.

When I initially woke up in the hospital, all I felt was relief. I believed God was there, and He saved me for a reason. At the time, I didn't know anyone was hurt besides me. The only thing I knew was I was in a horrific accident, and God saved me. Praise God! He is amazing! But as I stood in that line heading toward the Thunderdome, I started to think something totally different. Kanye West has a line in his song "Touched the Sky" where he says, "I think I died in that accident cause this must be heaven." He's referring to his superstardom after his near-fatal car accident. On the other hand, I started thinking the opposite. I started to question if I had died and gone to hell. I literally began to think, "Wait, did I actually die during the accident? Is this some alternate reality or existence. Am I living in hell? Is this God's punishment for not living a good life?" That's how bad the feeling and the situation were to me.

It started with hearing the words "double murder" and now, I was headed to the Thunderdome to face impending danger. I was headed to the second floor, the 2000 floor of the Men's County Jail in downtown Los Angeles. These cells are where they keep the worst

Inmate walking line at men's central jail

of the worst. But I was not the worst of the worst and God knew that. So why was he putting me there? God must have given up on me. He didn't care about me anymore. So, at that moment, as we are going into the Thunderdome, I made the decision I might have to die there because nobody was going to take anything from me. I have never been a punk and I was not going to be one of those people other inmates disrespect. I was determined to lay it all on the line when it came to respect. If death was the consequence, then so be it.

As I looked around, I realized if this is what my life was going to be like from that point on, then maybe death was a better option. It was the first time in my life I ever felt that way. It actually took away a lot of the fear of death. Even now, I still have many of those feelings. If I had a choice between the rest of my life in there versus death, I would choose death every day of the week and twice on Sundays.

It was so dark with cell block after cell block. It felt as if I was locked under the earth. There were no windows or clocks anywhere. You have no sense of time at all. And you have no idea who they would put you in a cell with.

2400 Cell Block (The Thunderdome)

As I was entering the 2400 cell block, I heard voices yelling out, "Who's that down there blood? Who's that down there cuzz? Where are you from? Yeah, when the showers open up we gonna be down there to see who that is!"

I was placed in a cell with a young Latino dude, "Shooter." I later found out he was in there for two murders and two attempted murders. Whenever you walk into a cell in the county, everybody wants to see what type of dude you are. They're trying to figure out whether or not you're a murderer or one of the bums off the street because you never know how long you will have to live with that person. It was a four-man cell. Shooter, the young Latino dude, didn't seem like a problem. There was also an older dude in there. The situation just seemed pretty cool with the people I was sharing a cell with. It wasn't what I had heard so far.

In the cell next to me, they wanted to know who I was. They yelled out, "Hey, Shooter, who's that in there? Is he a Black?" That means a Black man. Shooter yelled out, "Yeah." Then they said, "Hey, Black, what's your name?" I went to the cell entrance so they can hear me and told them my name. Then they asked the number one question that's asked every day and all day in the county, "Where are you from?" At that point, I didn't know what to say because I'm from Inglewood, and that has a stigma already. Inglewood is mostly a "Blood" city.

I was conflicted because I lived in Granada Hills, but I was not from Granada Hills. If I had said I was from Granada Hills, they would feel, "Ah man, this nigga's a valley nigga with no hood in him." So I just said to myself that from that point on I was going to be 100 percent honest and whatever happened, just happened. I didn't care anymore. I said, "I'm from Inglewood."

They said, "Where in Inglewood?"

I said, "The Bottoms."

And without hesitation, they responded, "Oh, you from Crenshaw Mafia."

I said, "Nope. I'm not a gangbanger, but I'm from Inglewood, The Bottoms."

After that, they were like, "Alright, bro."

I saw lots of other people's interactions go way worse than that. But mine didn't. I wasn't in there on some super tough stuff. It would've been stupid for me to say I was "Automatik from The Bottoms" with my chest poked out. I said, "I'm Rodney, and I'm from Inglewood but I'm not a gangbanger" because I wasn't. The tone of my voice wasn't some super, tough tone either. It was just some authentic man stuff. And that was my attitude in jail. I'm just a man in here, and I will not be anything more and definitely not anything less. I walked a fine line. I would not proclaim to be something I wasn't and act as if I was looking for problems. But at the same time, I wasn't going to behave as if I was running from problems because I would get labeled as soft and have problems anyway. It was a delicate balance for survival. Honestly, other guys were approached the same way I was and they got opposite reactions. I look back now and I realize that God was protecting me. To act as if I were some sort of gladiator would be my failure to acknowledge God's hand on me during my time in prison. That would be fake and I will never do that.

Those types of interactions with inmates were prevalent and constant. They happened everywhere: visiting time, going to see the nurse, and in the hallways. People would stare at you, study every move, and look at every tattoo. That type of interaction never dies down because there's so much movement, and new people are constantly coming and going. Every time someone enters the cellblock, the number one question is, "Where are you from?" It started to irritate me because I recognized we were all in there fighting for our lives against the real enemy—the system. Why was there so much emphasis on fighting each other?

It was August 6, 2017, when I first entered processing, and three days later, from that point, I was housed in the 2400 block of MCJ, the Thunderdome. Two days after I entered my cell in the 2400 block, I was able to take a shower. The cell itself was small probably about 8 x 5 feet and had no windows, no fresh air. There were four rows—A for Abel, B for Baker, C for Charlie, and D for Denver. At the time, I was on Abel row where there weren't any televisions. The only reason TVs were there at all was because the actor Robert Downey Jr. bought them out of the kindness of his heart, after spending some time there when he was going through his legal issues.

I was in 2400 Abel #4. I will never forget. Once a week, they're supposed to let you go to the yard (outside), which in the county was on the roof. However, the roof is covered with a thick plastic net; it's depressing. The entire time I was in 2400 (six weeks), I never went to the roof for sunlight and air. I was also supposed to get a shower twice a week, but they would take away these types of privileges, like going to the yard and showers, sometimes for no reason. So, if one person did something wrong, they would revoke privileges for everyone. The entire time I was in the Thunderdome, I didn't get any sunlight. But I learned that's part of what makes 2400 the Thunderdome.

Another aspect of the Thunderdome is you can hear everything happening in the cell next to you, and it messes up your mind. When they open up the cells for showers, the guys come down the line asking, "Where are you from? Oh, yeah, you got fades! You got enemies here, and you gotta fight." So, if you're from a certain gang and any of your main enemies are there, you have to fight them all. The officers and everybody knows about it; they're complicit. The gang representatives will let the officers know they have to "handle some business," and the guards walk off somewhere and let inmates fight during shower time. If there are five members from the same gang in there, and you're from the rival gang, you'll have five fades during shower time. That's called "getting ran." If somebody says he got ran in a particular part of the jail, that means he was forced to fight a lot of people in a row, most likely from his rival gang.

The other thing that you learn during shower time is how to wash yourself, your shirt, and your boxers at the same time when you shower. You don't want to be naked in the shower, so you wash up with your boxers on while simultaneously washing your boxers. You wash your clothes in the sink with bar soap. Then you air dry everything by making a makeshift clothesline in your cell. You're not supposed to even have a clothesline. When officers get upset, they come into your cell and rip the lines down. There's no washing machine or a cleaning service where they come and collect your clothes, clean them, and give them back. That lasted for six weeks.

Some people like the cells because they have fewer people to deal with. In the cell, at the most, you only have three other people in the same room with you, but in the dorms, you could be in the same room with 120 people. A dorm is just a big room with a whole bunch of bunk beds, a whole bunch of people, and a whole bunch of personalities. It's a whole bunch of different situations going on.

The cell kills your spirit. 2400 was like a dungeon. But in the dorms, there was no sunlight either. The only time I saw sunlight was when they transported me to court. But even on the bus, the windows are blacked out. The entire ordeal was torture. The process is deliberate. The intention is to break you. This system is set up to make that part of the process the worst to force people to settle for whatever deal the DA offered. Even if they're innocent, people will plead guilty to a charge just to end the county jail part of the process. Lawyers and district attorneys have 98 percent conviction rates because they put people in that situation, and they will do anything to make it end as fast as possible.

During the six weeks that I was on the 2400 block, I wasn't doing anything. I was just lying in the cell rotting. The first thing I did when I got money on my books was to buy a deck of cards. I must have played solitaire thousands of times. The food in jail was slop or mush, so you're coerced into buying food like Top Ramen noodles, a delicacy in jail.

They charge you five times more for everything. I don't think you could survive just eating the food they give you in jail. It's slavery. The messed-up thing is in this country, you are supposedly innocent until proven guilty, but while you're waiting in jail for your court case, you're treated as if you are guilty. Even if you're innocent, you'll say you're guilty just to get out of there faster. That's how many innocent people ended up with criminal records. As I said, processing was the worst three days in my life out of everything I endured, including ICU, the arrest, and the penitentiary.

County jail food

The six weeks I spent in 2400 take second place. You are constantly on guard. Loud sounds and screams come from the cells right next to you, and it takes a toll on your mind. You also hear about people dying while in there. But my mindset at that time was if they tell me this is where I will be for the next fifteen years then death would be better. I was prepared to get jumped by eight guys versus letting anyone disrespect me, which could happen at any time.

When I was younger, I had a romantic idea of what jail was, and I didn't care as much about consequences. Now, my perspective is much clearer. I'm much more thoughtful about situations that could take me away from my family and put me in situations like that again.

Quamé: What was the Thunderdome like? What did it look and feel like? What sort of things/events did you witness while there? Did it live up to its name or was it more hyped up?

Rodney: The Thunderdome definitely lived up to the hype. When you are a criminal or a tough guy of any kind in LA, surviving there is where you get your name in the streets. It will make you or break you. It's gladiator school. What you have done in the streets or how intense your war is with that particular rival gang will determine what will happen. For a while, they were acting as if they were giving people fair fights then they would stab them. As I said earlier, the guards allow all of this to go on. The reps would tell the guards, "Aye, we need to handle our business in this cell; go to the other side for fifteen minutes," and they would.

Thunderdome will bring the man out of you. All I knew was that I wasn't going to let anyone take anything from me, even if it meant death. People were dying while I was in there, and nobody cared. To me, it was the closest thing to hell. I've seen people come in with gang tattoos all over their faces, acting super tough, but they folded and rolled it up. In other words, they asked to be moved to a different facility because they feared for their lives.

The LA County jail is the worst place to do time. And at the time, 2400 was the worst place in the county jail. It's run by gangs. It is all about separation by race. It is set up that way by the system. It's inhumane and in a state of chaos and should totally be revamped.

CHAPTER 12

5200 – THE SCHOOL DORM

How I got moved to the school dorm is an interesting story. The trustees from the school dorm walk by the cells on 2400 every few weeks or so and yell out, "Is anyone interested in going to school?" I heard Shooter, my cellmate, who had been there for months say, "Man, I put in for school like four times. Man, they never call nobody from down here." But something told me to sign up anyway. So, I did.

Two days later, the deputy yelled out, "Wright, roll it up, you're moving to the school dorm!"

My cellmates said, "What?! Wait a minute! Hey, man, we've been down here for months, and they haven't called us!" I gathered all my paperwork and everything I had accumulated to take up the stairs to the 5000 floor, dorm 5200. As I was walking down the fifth floor through this long hallway, the very first thing I saw was the chapel where they have church services. We had nothing like that on 2400. For me, it was a small sign that God was saying I haven't forgotten you; this is just another part of the deliverance process. When I entered the dorm, guys greeted me and said, "What's up?" and "Where are you from?" (of course). In the dorm, there was more comradery within your race, whereas, in 2400, I was down there by myself with the wolves.

The dorm wasn't summer camp either, and race was more of a determining factor in your experience. As a Black man, other Blacks let me know who cut hair, and they offered me little things I needed like soap and books, or whatever. The best thing about dorm living was that the shower was accessible 24 hours and you didn't have to wait a week to clean yourself. I was able to shave with the little, cheap razors that broke out my skin but, at least, I could shave. That's when I realized how vital simple luxuries like washing and grooming myself could affect my mental state. I had a small feeling of hope just from having these allowances on 5200, the school dorm. I did the majority of my time in the county jail in 5200 (eighteen and a half months). I spent a month and a half in 2400.

While in 5200, information started to come in about my case. My lawyer informed me of the toxicology report. My blood alcohol was 0.16, which is twice the legal limit. But there was nothing else in my system. The police had done a toxicology report and my lawyer had also gotten one done. They both said the same thing– just alcohol.

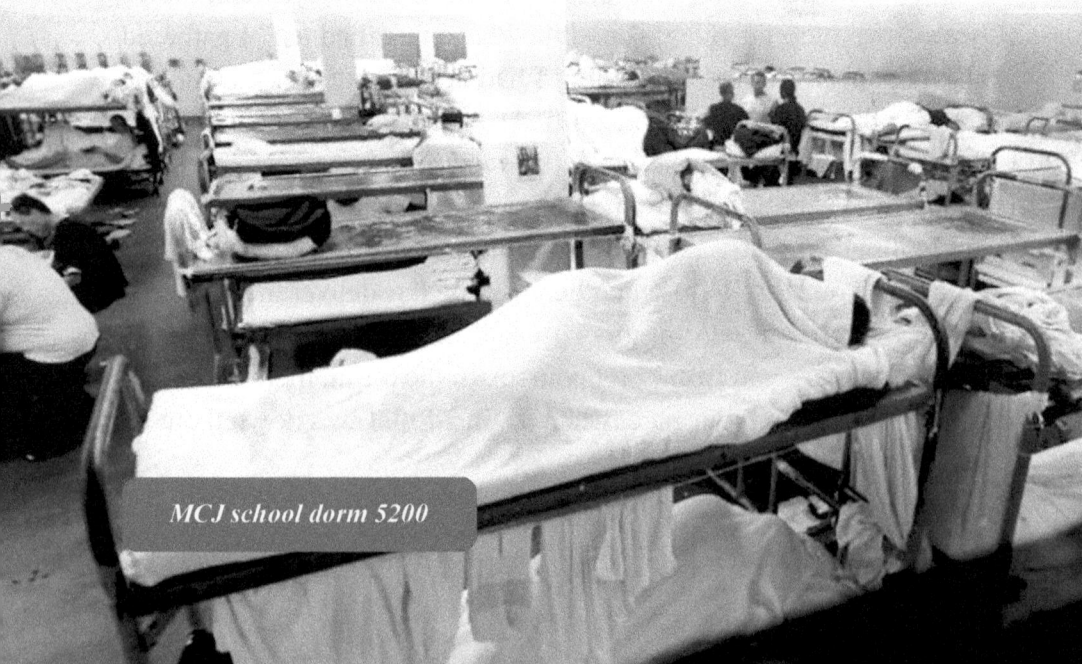

MCJ school dorm 5200

I was really confused. I started thinking, "Maybe I didn't take a piece of any pill that night." But it just really did not make sense. I was a drinker. I went out a lot and drank way heavier drinks than wine. Never before did I even get as much as a speeding ticket when driving. How could a few glasses of wine cause me to be doing something as crazy as driving the wrong way on the freeway? While in jail, I believe God sent me confirmation. I came across a few different people who did drugs and popping pills was their thing. While talking to these people just in regular conversation they would get into stories about taking Xanax. One story, in particular, stood out to me.

In 5200, I was talking to one of my boys I used to play cards with. Out of the blue, he went into a story about a time when he had one drink and took a Xanax pill at one of his closest friends' houses. He said he woke up at the house of his ex-girlfriend whom he hadn't talked to in a while. Then he said he went to his friend's house where he was the night before to ask him what had happened because he couldn't remember. When he got there, his friend was furious and said he never wanted to have anything to do with him again. He asked why. The friend told him the night before that he started an argument for no reason that ended up with him pulling a gun on his friend and his friend's girlfriend. He said he didn't remember anything about that story. Consequently, he did some research on Xanax and discovered it is a strong psyche med that causes blackouts when mixed with any amount of alcohol. He told me he did cocaine, crystal meth, and every pill you can imagine, even Xanax, but he said he would never mix Xanax with any alcohol again. I also heard a couple of other blackout stories from people while I was there. That was confirmation for me.

When I got out of jail, I looked up Xanax. Here's what it said, "A controlled substance that can cause paranoid or suicidal ideation and impair memory. Combining with other substances, particularly alcohol, can slow breathing and possibly lead to death." Also, in bold, were the words, "Avoid alcohol: Very serious interactions can occur" (understatement). Honestly, I don't believe the toxicology report. When I needed to sleep so I could function at work the next day, I would take a quarter of one of those pills and after 20-30 minutes, they would kick in, and I would be out cold. I would wake up refreshed, no matter how much sleep I had.

I had never taken them outside of the house. However, that night, realizing it was late and I had to get up for work that morning, at some point on the way home, I took a quarter of that Xanax pill, thinking by the time I got home, it would kick in and I would go straight to sleep. What I didn't know was the danger of doing that. I did not know the side effects and what mixing Xanax with any amount of alcohol, even wine, could do.

> My people are destroyed for lack of knowledge.
> (Hosea 4:6)

Contrary to the world's term, "What you don't know can't hurt you," taking something I didn't know anything about caused such an extremely tragic event that changed my life and the lives of others forever. I was taking Xanax because I was sleep-deprived due to the stress, depression, and other issues in my life.

I heard a rap song on the radio the other day, and the lyrics were talking about "drinking henny, and poppin zannys." As someone who used to rap, I never agreed with censorship. But I had a change of heart. I was watching the news recently, and they were talking about when certain rappers got banned and were dropped from big endorsement deals because of offensive lyrics that were considered dangerous to a particular group. I couldn't help but think about all of the pistol poppin' and drug use in music that is allowed. Meanwhile, murder is at an all-time high, and drug overdoses continue to kill thousands of people daily. Yet, no one seems to care if that type of music is played on the radio for kids to hear. Anyway, that's a whole other book.

One of the first things I learned when I got to the school dorm was the disproportionate number of Black and Latino men in comparison to the small number of White men incarcerated. Yet, we are a way smaller part of the overall population in the state and the country. I noticed that as soon as I got to the dorm. Out of the 120 people in 5200 dorm, I would say on average, fifty were Black, fifty were Latino, ten were White, and the other ten were Asian.

I researched cases exactly like mine. There was one case, in Van Nuys, where a white man hit a Hispanic man as he was crossing the street. He took the police on a high-speed chase all the way to Palos Verde, and they had to use a spike strip to burst his tires to get him to stop. This man had alcohol, cocaine, and barbiturates in his system. He received a four-year suspended sentence. He was sentenced to complete a drug program. The key phrase in that story is "Palos Verde," the city where he lived (a very upper-class neighborhood in Southern California). I learned quickly that the system is all about race and more importantly, money.

CHAPTER 13

ACCEPTANCE AND ACCOUNTABILITY

Quamé: You talk about a healing phase that was happening during the first twenty months of going to jail where the theme of acceptance and apologizing occurred. Did it happen physically where you contacted specific people or was it to whoever was in your face? How did it happen?

Rodney: Yes. I had to reach out to most people. For example, Nicole, my ex-wife, I always felt she was kind of crazy. She flies off the handle, is irrational, and goes way overboard at times, but I realize now I caused a lot of that behavior. She was a good girl, but her reaction to the stuff I was doing, made her look crazy. While in the county jail, she was one of the first people I reached out and apologized to. I wrote her a letter from prison and apologized for tearing up our family with my arrogance, galivanting, and all of that.

Quamé: Did she write you back?

Rodney: Yeah, she wrote me back. I didn't get an apology though, but that's okay. Lots of wrong things were done to me, but two wrongs don't make a right. I was the person who started the wrong behavior and anything after that was just a response to what I did. Although I did not get the apology I expected, I did my part.

I apologized to her and Cherisse. I still have a lot of apologizing to do to people, especially the women I've come across in my life. I admit I was doing a lot and people's feelings got hurt.

Quamé: Did you write Cherisse a letter too or did you reach out to her?

No, I did not write her a letter. I called and talked to her. She was accepting and was still willing to be there for me. She's a very good-hearted person. She accepted my apology and said, "Whatever you need, I got you." But I had to grow mentally with her because she is so kind-hearted, it can easily turn into manipulation if you give false hope. That was also a part of my 20-month process of growth in the county jail. I learned that certain actions and the little things we say as men can give false hope, even if we don't mean to.

She said, "Hey, apology accepted and whatever you need. As a matter of fact, I'll come visit you and if you need anything on your books I got you." I had to really pray about the situation and trust God to provide for me. I did not want in the least bit to lead her on or take advantage of her kindness in any way. But for most people in jail, that's how they survive. They have multiple women, and they prey on the women's emotions to get the stuff that they need. I had to make the decision, not to even remotely play with her heart or anything like that. I had to be honest, even if it meant going without. I was not going to string her along.

Quamé: At that time, you were already in the middle of your relationship with Tottie, and you had a new baby girl. But I would imagine that being in your situation, you could easily catch emotions involuntarily if someone is being that supportive and kind.

Rodney: Yes, and for a while, I was confused because I have known her for years. I realized in new relationships, you will experience certain faults in your new partner, and it's human nature to compare and say, "Well, the last person doesn't have those specific faults." That may cause you to start comparing people. So, I had to clearly make a decision. I also had to tell Cherisse during a surprise visit not to come anymore.

Cherisse started crying when I told her that. Then during a phone call, she said I had become the man she always wanted me to be, but I became that for someone else. That was crazy to hear, but I see now it was the truth.

Quamé: What do you do when someone tells you that, and you are behind bars so you have to sit with it? What are you sitting with when someone tells you that?

Rodney: First of all, in jail, you have to disconnect from your surroundings. Not doing so is the dumbest thing, although the people in there try to convince you otherwise. The few people I told that Cherisse wanted to be there for me said, "Man, you're crazy." "You should let her." "So, are you purposely narrowing down your livelihood to one person, an emotional woman at that,

MCJ's visiting room

who if she gets mad at you can say, 'to hell with you' and then you have nobody?" That makes a lot of sense and I sound a little crazy as I think about it now, especially when I reflect on how Tottie can be sometimes. But that's where my belief in God and His promises came in. My belief was not in Tottie; it was in God. To be perfectly honest, that was very hard for me to do. I'm the type of person who always has a backup plan, but when Cherisse came and offered whatever I needed, I told her I didn't need anything. The culture on the inside is to keep as many women as you possibly can in case one falls off (as they often do), you will always have another to pick up the slack. Makes sense, doesn't it? But I was living by faith. God told me to do it this way, and He will not leave me hanging.

Quamé: You were battling all these other voices inside the pen saying otherwise. But was there any OG that confirmed what God was telling you?

Rodney: No, not at all! It was so bad I stopped talking to people about it. Nobody could say worst than what was going on in my own head about the situation anyway. It was a real inner battle, but it was the right thing to do. I was connected spiritually more than I had ever been in my life. Being obedient to God was more important to me than anything. It all worked out just as He promised. God didn't leave me hanging at all. Neither did Tottie. In county, you get 2 visits a week. Tottie visited me twice every week. I met people in there for years that maybe got one or two visits from loved ones. Visits, cards, and letters are huge to people doing time. Hearing your name at mail call can get you through the next month without losing your mind. Tottie did all of those things and WAY more. She attended every court date. When I was moved to prison, she drove hours to visit me. We talked and prayed on the phone every night until my release. She will always have my heart. She could actually have my heart if hers was to fail. She is my angel and my rock!

Quamé: You're a spiritual man, and I see your spirituality is based on discipline and faith. You can't have faith without discipline.

Rodney: Everything that happened came through faith. Not faith in my money, not faith in my lawyer, not faith in a woman, not faith in my own strength, but it was faith in God and what His Word says.

> And without faith it is impossible to please God,
> because anyone who comes to him must believe that
> he exists and that he rewards those who earnestly
> seek him. (Hebrews 11:6)

In a situation like mine, all you have is faith, but faith is enough.

Quamé: But faith is unseen. You had something tangible in a woman who was offering to support you but you chose something unseen.

Rodney: Exactly! That's why it was so hard. However, I learned that you have what you believe in. You can't see it because it hasn't manifested yet, but God says it's there. It's our job to keep speaking it and believing we have it, even though we can't see it yet. We should declare, "This will happen. As a matter of fact, it has already happened. It just hasn't appeared yet."

> Now faith is the substance of things hoped for, the
> evidence of things not seen. (Hebrews 11:1)

Through belief and patience, you will slowly but surely watch it manifest. This process taught me that. It's like when you post something in the mail, and the postal service says you will get it tomorrow before noon. Because you trust the postal service, you go on with your day and live as if the package is already there, even though it hasn't arrived yet. If we have that much faith in the postal service, how much more faith should we have in God.

It's weird because I was very spiritually connected when I was in jail. However, now that I am out when tests come, and I try to tap in as I did while in jail, it's more difficult now because I am surrounded by the world and more naysayers. Scripture says we are more connected when we are going through trials and tribulations.

> My brethren, count it all joy when you fall into various
> trials, knowing that the testing of your faith produces
> patience. But let patience have its perfect work, that
> you may be perfect and complete, lacking nothing.
> (James 1:2-4)

But who wants to go through trials and tribulations? None of us because they hurt. Therefore, our connection to God is usually not as strong as it is in the storm. I guess I'm trying to stay connected without having to go through a painful storm.

Quamé: The theme we're talking about is acceptance and accountability. It sounds like you're embracing the trials and tribulations you're in at this point while in jail.

Rodney: Yes, I am embracing them, but it is very difficult. Nobody wants trials and tribulations. The truth is I learned more about God and myself during the trials and tribulations, and my faith grew because He promised not to leave me while I was in the storm. He said He would deliver me from it. He did

> God has said, "Never will I leave you; never will I
> forsake you." (Hebrews 13:5b NIV)

I discovered later that at the heart of my entire situation was depression combined with dishonesty and not dealing with situations head-on. It took me a while to come to that understanding in the county jail.

Here's a good example of how depression and my dishonesty were confirmed in jail. One of my favorite movies is "A Thin Line between Love and Hate" starring Martin Lawrence. I loved this movie because Martin's character is a player, and he's funny. However, for some reason, when I watched it in jail, I had a different perspective.

Martin's character, a player, came across a crazy woman who tried to kill him for breaking her heart. In the end, Martin goes to her house after she burns down the club where he works. She hits him over the head and tells him to get into the tub so she can electrocute him. Martin yells, "I'm not getting in no tub." So, she shoots him, and he falls into the tub. As she is about to kill him, she asks, "Do you have anything else you want to say, Mr. Player?"

Martin responds, "Yeah, I apologize!"

Immediately something said to me, "Do you realize throughout this entire movie, this is the first time he apologized for the things he did to her?" It took all of that devastation, stalking him, damaging his car, and burning down his club, but he never thought to apologize until she was about to take his life. Immediately after he apologized, the woman had a look of slight remorse on her face and subsequently, he was delivered from the life-threatening situation. That spoke to me. It confirmed what I had already been thinking. I had caused all of this drama and never once apologized to any of the people I hurt.

I was mad at Nicole, my first wife, for being mad at me for my dishonesty. Was she wrong in her actions? Yes, the woman who was stalking and trying to kill Martin in the movie was also wrong. However, if he had apologized from the start, he probably wouldn't have gone through such trauma to the point of almost dying. I should have been straight up with Nicole from the start. I should have told her I had another child on the way and there was no possibility of us getting back together. Perhaps she would have moved on with her life and may not have attacked me the way she did. She might have been mad initially but would have probably respected my honesty.

At that point in jail, I took responsibility for my actions and admitted I caused everything. But before I came to this realization, I was in denial and disbelief. I kept offering myself and everyone excuses for why and how the collision happened. No matter how valid some of my excuses may have been, they were still excuses. So, I had to man up and take full responsibility.

The DA and the family of the victims didn't care why and what the circumstances were surrounding the accident. My response to their two children being gone can't be a bunch of excuses—"I didn't mean to do it." "I only drank wine." "I was depressed." The family could not care less about all that! They want to know if I understand the extent of what I did. They want to know if I am remorseful. But thankfully, it clicked for me before the sentencing and that's what I did. I apologized. I can't make amends for the death of their two sons, but I can change. I can be different and try to help other people. I know sorry is not enough in this situation. I accept full responsibility.

A lot of people thought a ten-year sentence was too much time for someone with no previous record or malicious intent involved in the crime. However, I didn't want to put the family through another day of litigation. I don't remember everything I said verbatim because I spoke to the family from the heart. From what I hear, the family received my words. I believe that started the restoration process for me. However, the lessons I've learned continued through the people God sent to speak to me in prison. Arrogance and dishonesty were a big part of my downfall.

My attitudes and actions caused the women in my life to react the way they did. Thus, I suffered from depression, which caused insomnia, which all led up to that night. But the night of the accident, God said:

> Enough is enough; you're not heeding My warnings. Go and sit down and learn My Word. Go and learn how to be the husband and father I called you to be. Go and unlearn the ways of the world. Learn My ways and live by them. When I remove all of the blessings I gave you, which you had the nerve to think you got on your own, and you have suffered enough and been humbled, I will give them back to you and double. And when I miraculously deliver you from this situation and send you back to the world better than before, tell people about what I did for you and I can do it for them too.

God humbled me. He tore down the entire persona I had built. The arrogant "Auto" I had created, God dismantled in one night. But God didn't deem me useless because I'm still here.

We are not sensitive to depression in the Black community at all. In my family, if you have something going on that's difficult to handle, people will tell you to suck it up and be tough. Plus, in my situation, I've always been the person other people would call on for advice. I tried to talk to my grandmother on my dad's side once. I told her I had a bunch of stuff going on with the women in my life, my children, and so forth, and I didn't know how to handle it. I'll never forget her response. It was, "You know; you just bought some income property; just keep doing that kind of stuff. Keep buying real estate, working hard, and everything will work out."

I love and respect my grandmother but that didn't help me at all because money or success does not bring peace, and there's no man-made cure for depression. Whatever your vice is, it won't heal the heart and bring you peace. I just wanted peace. Where could I find peace? It wasn't at home at the time, so I didn't want to go home. I tried to find it by going out and partying. But that only brought me temporary relief. It only numbed the pain temporarily, but it wasn't fixing the situation. Now, I have learned to face things head-on in prayer and then in action. Whatever happens, happens; that's part of the healing process.

Only God can bring you peace. If I was more in tune and had a relationship with God, instead of just being a "church-goer," I believe everything would have been different. I was in a dark place, but I am in a way better place than I was then. The irony is that financially, I was doing the best I had ever done. I had just bought my second property. I owned a three-unit building in Los Angeles at the time. I had just received a promotion, and I was at an all-time high at work, earning well over six figures but still at the lowest point of my life somehow.

I suffered in silence because it is taboo to bring up depression in the Black community. Plus, financially, I was doing better than most people around me at the time, so they didn't want to hear about my so-called "issues." They were focused more on my material success, so their response was, "Bro, you're blessed, while I'm over here facing *real* issues. You just bought another house, and I'm worried about how I'm going to pay my rent where I live!" When I received responses like that while talking to people, I pulled back and suppressed it. Suppression is not a healthy alternative. In fact, it is the worst thing you can do because eventually, the issue will come to the surface in some way.

I would suck it up, go out, and be Automatik because people liked "Auto." I had to be "Auto" at all costs. Nobody cared about Rodney's issues. As much as they hurt, I had to keep going and hoped they would just go away. Look what that thinking cost me. People at work knew Rodney, but Auto was more attractive; it was like an alter ego. It wasn't healthy though; it was depressing.

The more I reflect, the more I realize how amazing God is because He didn't just put me in jail; it wasn't just a punishment. When I was moved up to the school dorm for the next $18^{1/2}$ months, I took several classes–substance absence, child development, anger management, and other classes. I learned about trauma and the different categorizations and levels of trauma. I learned I ranked almost at the highest level of childhood trauma. According to the research, I ranked at level 6, and it said people who ranked level 4 and up should receive extensive therapy. The only people higher than those at my level were people who had extreme issues like sexual abuse.

Another study was done that revealed children who grew up in South Central Los Angeles at the time I did had PTSD levels equivalent to children growing up in war-torn areas in Iraq. So, simply growing up where I did was itself traumatic. I recognize that now because I live in Granada Hills. One day, I was at the gas station down the street from my home. A White guy and I were standing there pumping our gas. A car suddenly pulled into the gas station so fast the tires screeched. Immediately, I ducked and braced myself. The guy across from me didn't even blink. He kinda chuckled and asked me if I was okay. I explained to him that where I'm from, shots usually followed tires screeching. That confirmed to me the difference between people who grew up in South Central LA and those who grew up in more affluent areas. I believe if I had counseling or therapy or someone to talk to at the time, the entire situation would probably not have happened. But when those options are not available to you or you are not aware those options can help, then you do what most people do: self-medicate.

I wish none of this had happened and those two men didn't lose their lives. However, if my actions from this point on can prevent others from being in a similar situation, that's the good that may come out of this. James says:

> My brethren, count it all joy when you fall into
> various trials, knowing that the testing of your faith
> produces patience. (James 1:2-3)

When I first read that passage, I was in the county jail. I shut the Bible and said, "Man, why would I ever count these trials as joy?" I learned God was dealing with me. I could have been dead.

The closest you get to God is when you're broken. When you're successful and feeling good, you think you don't need God. You might thank God for what you have, but you feel you're in charge and you have everything under control. However, when you're broken and you don't have anybody to call on but God, you draw close to Him. And that's when God says, "Good, I was waiting for you to get here. Now, let Me deliver you and lift you up. That's what I wanted to do the entire time, but you've been so far away, thinking you have it all under control, not understanding you need Me."

> And call on me in the day of trouble; I will deliver
> you, and you will honor me. (Psalm 50:15 NIV)

In jail, I was calling out to God like never before because nothing else was going to work. The lawyers and money didn't have the answer. No one knew how my court case would go. God was the only One who could help me. The testimony from all of this would touch and affect more than just myself. That's what is meant by counting it all joy because a lot of good would come from it. Ironically, that's what the father of the two men who died in the accident said to my family in the hallway after my sentencing: "I just want to see the good that comes out of this."

CHAPTER 14

THE COURT PROCEEDINGS AND FINAL SENTENCING

There was no trial, I just pled guilty. You would think it would be open and shut, but it wasn't. Sometimes, the charges against you are much greater than what the situation is, and your lawyer has to work to bring them down to ones that are more comparable to your actual circumstances. For the first nine months, the prosecution never mentioned anything about a deal, and it appeared that they were pursuing the maximum charges of double murder. My lawyer said they weren't returning his calls and we may have to go to trial. They finally offered a deal of twelve years with 80 percent (serving nine years). My immediate reaction was, "Twelve years for my first felony that was unintentional?" My lawyer explained it was because people lost their lives, but he went on to say he didn't think I should accept that deal. Hence, the process was extended by months. It was twenty months before I received my final sentence. This is why the first twenty months were hell. I didn't know how long I would be imprisoned. It was mental torture and draining.

The final court appearance and sentencing were hard. I had to face the family of the two men who lost their lives in the accident for the first time. That's where the themes of acceptance and accountability became salient. I stood in front of the family and told them what I wanted to tell them from day one. I told them I was very, very, sorry, and I didn't mean it. I knew the process was harder on them than even on me.

The district attorney talked to the family periodically to let them know if they would offer me a certain amount of time to avoid a trial. Of course, the family's first response, I heard, was "I can't believe you're going to offer him anything." They were grieving the loss of their loved ones. The family felt I should go to jail for the rest of my life. I understood that initial response. But within those twenty months, the district attorney presented the offer to the family. We settled on ten years with 50 percent of the time needed to be served. At the final sentencing, I had the option of saying something to the family or not. I chose to say something. I was going to write it down, but I felt reading to them wasn't right, so I chose to speak from the heart. I didn't know how the family would receive my words or if they would receive them at all. I had heard horror stories about sentencing hearings and what took place, so I didn't know what to expect.

The two men who died were brothers, so there was only one family and they had to mourn the loss of two children at the same time. I heard that their father was the one who went to the morgue to identify his two sons. That is the bravest thing I have ever heard and I don't think I am man enough to do that. By the grace of God, the family went from "To hell with him; he should get life" to showing up at the sentencing with a different mindset. There wasn't any bashing. Their sister spoke on behalf of their family and requested I use my time in prison wisely. And upon my release, use my life to speak to people to prevent tragedies like these from happening to other people. I made a promise to them I would do that.

Once the COVID-19 situation clears up a bit, I plan to go to Driving Under the Influence (DUI) classes to speak to people. One thing many don't know is once you receive a DUI, you are required to sign a document that acknowledges you can be charged with murder if you're involved in an accident and someone dies. I met multiple people in jail with life sentences because that was their exact situation. What could've been vehicular manslaughter became murder because they had a previous DUI and had signed that document. This applies even if the accident is not your fault.

I met a guy in jail who was driving under the influence, and another car made a left turn in front of him and caused the accident. He hit them and they died. The driver of the car he hit was also under the influence. Even though the report ruled he had the right of way, he was facing life in jail because it was his second DUI. Fortunately for me, I didn't have a previous DUI, and that was a huge factor in my case.

The family never said they forgave me. I was told that after I spoke, they left the courtroom and prayed with my family in the hallway. I pray my words gave them some type of peace and closure. I know they may never reach complete closure, but through my actions, I will do my best to ensure the lives of their loved ones will not be in vain.

CHAPTER 15

EPIPHANIES IN JAIL

Quamé: What were the top five things you learned about yourself in jail?

1. I learned my rightful position and role in my household and family.

2. I learned the morals that I adopted from my environment are backward when compared to godly morals.

3. I learned how important I am to many people and what a great responsibility that is.

4. I learned I was arrogant and not as good a person as I thought I was.

5. I learned I owe a lot of people apologies because of my actions.

Quamé: Okay, so the first thing you said you learned was your rightful position and role in your household and you family. So, what is that position? And was there an epiphany? Was there any specific moment that solidified that thought, or did it come to you over a period of time?

Rodney: It was kind of an epiphany. I learned a lot in the county jail from going to the Bible studies. The Bible says husbands are the heads of their wives

> For the husband is head of the wife, as also Christ is head of the church; and He is the Savior of the body.
> (Ephesians 5:23).

There is a particular order. God put men as the heads of the family, but not as some men may interpret it as "ruling over women."

Women are equal to men in their positions, but we have different roles. For example, let's say two people started a company and they are both equal shareowners; they both own 50 percent. However, one person handles the business aspect and the other person handles the production. So. one person becomes the head of the business or administrative aspects and the other person is the head of production. If a big business decision must be made, the person who is the head of business would make that call. However, for the business to succeed, both partners are equally important. I learned I'm the head. I'm important and I have roles. As the head, I have more responsibilities; I have no time to waste or be childish anymore. The saying goes, "Heavy is the head that wears the crown."

When I was a child, I spoke as a child, I understood as a child, I thought as a child; but when I became a man, I put away childish things. (1 Corinthians 13:11)

Tottie and me at my Career Education Program graduation – LA Men's Central Jail – 2018

You must grow up. I had to grow up. My childish behavior created a mess in my life. Even though I was the king of my household, I wasn't maneuvering as a king should. I was placed as the king of my castle, but I was still running around like a court jester. That revelation brought growth.

I believe God put me through this trying time to sit me down and train me. He made me better before He put me back into the world. God is not going to put someone back into the world unchanged because that's not the purpose of such a trying situation. In multiple places in the Bible, it speaks about the refining process.

> Behold, I have refined you, but not as silver; I have tested you in the furnace of affliction. (Isaiah 48:10).

I kept hearing about that in jail. Well, I learned that in the process of purifying gold, they put it in extreme heat. When put in the heat or the refining fire, the impurities in the gold rise to the surface to be scraped off. This once flawed gold is now purified and more valuable. I discovered many of us have deep-rooted impurities: drug habits, alcoholism, greed, lust for money or the opposite sex, or whatever the particular vice is that causes you to be impure. Everything that is not of God, which we pick up from the world–the hood, environment, or dysfunctional family–is an impurity.

When God wants to promote you, He first purifies you. He gets all of the impurities from the world out of you. His fire is affliction (jail, a sickness, the death of someone close, job loss) or whatever it takes for you to call on Him and Him only. If you are the piece of gold in the fire, you are screaming, "God, please get me out of here; this hurts!" But He leaves you in there longer because you don't realize there are still impurities in you that haven't come to the surface yet. Once I got that epiphany, in hindsight, the rest of my time in jail was the training. The epiphany answered the question, why am I here?

I used to wonder about all the relationships I admittedly ruined, but a lot of wrongs were done to me also. I would wonder why I was the only one in jail. Why was I the only one going through difficulties? Why were the ones who did me wrong (my ex-wife) allowed to move on with life? But after my epiphany and training, I knew I was the head and heavy is the head.

Quamé: Were you sitting in a cell with three other cats when you had that epiphany? Were you writing a letter when you had that epiphany? Were you already in the dorm?

Rodney: I was living in the school dorm when I had that epiphany. At that time, I was trying to figure out the purpose in all of this and why a good God allowed me to be in jail. I was going to church on Sunday. I was going to Bible study on Tuesday, Wednesday, and Thursday. I was going to all of them because I needed to hear God speak. I didn't want to miss anything because I didn't know where God's message was going to come from. I was trying to put myself in the best place and position to receive His word to me. It came at one of the Bible studies.

Quamé: Were you a churchgoer before?

Rodney: Yes. And that's one of the reasons I questioned why God would put me through all of this. Most of the people I know don't go to church or even care about the church. They were moving through life like me and even worse, but God wasn't putting them through anything. Yet, I was the one going through hell. I didn't understand that. But the epiphanies enlightened me and showed me my purpose. I had to lead my family in the direction God wanted me to.

> Do not be deceived, God is not mocked; for whatever a man sows, that he will also reap. For he who sows to his flesh will of the flesh reap corruption,

but he who sows to the Spirit will of the Spirit reap everlasting life. And let us not grow weary while doing good, for in due season we shall reap if we do not lose heart. (Galatians 6:7-9)

I also learned about sowing and reaping. What did I sow? I sowed a lot of hatred, resentment, and dishonesty. When you get back what you sow, you can't be mad. When this epiphany came to me, I thought of an analogy.

If you say something to somebody kind of disrespectful and then they hit you, most people are going to be worried about being hit and they're going to feel some way about being hit. A more mature person will first look at themselves and question what they said that provoked being hit.

In the situation with my ex-wife, I was dishonest. I didn't realize what I was sowing. Then my ex-wife lied to the court about child support and said I didn't support my children for ten years. I was hurt by that. I reacted by saying to myself she was a horrible, dishonest person. I did not look inside to see my part in the situation or question what I did to piss her off like that. I lied, cheated, and did all kinds of wickedness, but I could not see myself. For a long time, I only focused on her actions, not my own–until I was in jail. I sowed dishonesty and I reaped exactly what I sowed.

I also learned how important I am to my entire family. I heard this first and foremost from the people in my household but also from cousins and friends, years later, who told me my absence really hurt them. They said not being able to call and talk to me affected them greatly. They told me I was the bar they were shooting for. That shocked me because I didn't know I was a role model to other grown men, some of them years older than me. I didn't know people were watching and looking at me as an example. I was just living life and making the best decisions I possibly could. But role model– I didn't think so.

Quamé: Why didn't you realize that?

Rodney: I don't know. I was just moving too fast I guess. I was making moves I thought were good. A lot of them turned out positively, but I thought everyone was doing the same. I had lots of conversations with people, but I didn't know my advice meant so much to them. I was speaking from the heart. I didn't know my absence would affect their lives to the extent that it did. I knew it would affect my children and my girls' lives but not my cousins and friends. I only found that out when I got to the halfway house and was able to get a cell phone. People were calling me and letting me know how much they missed me. I have a cousin who I would go to the mall with, and he said he didn't go to the mall the entire time I was gone because that was our routine. That tripped me out.

I was arrogant and stubborn. One's fall or humbling process is based on how stubborn one is. It's like when you chastise your children. You know which child must be punished for a month versus a couple of days. A couple of days for one child may be nothing. He would probably say, "I can do that standing on my head," and nothing changes. While another child may be devastated by a three-day punishment and will never commit an offense again. I must have been very stubborn and hardheaded to get such a humbling experience.

Quamé: Respond to how the morals you learned in your home and social environment were backward to truly godly morals.

Rodney: As I was learning God's Word in jail, I wanted more and more because it was the truth. Having found the truth, I discerned the lies I received from my environment. Although I was going to church before jail, I was exactly that–a "church-goer." I wasn't practicing the core principles of Christ. Honestly, I thought people were supposed to simply go to church on Sunday and that was sufficient. But my circumstances taught me the process is much deeper than simply going to church. It's the same idea that going to school doesn't equate to learning. You must have the desire to learn, soak up the knowledge, and apply it. If that isn't the case, then why are you attending school?

Everything is backward. The world's standards for living are contrary to God's Word and instructions. One of the examples I spoke about was relationships. In middle school (when you really start liking girls) if you liked a girl too much you would get clowned. And you definitely couldn't say you loved her. Step back and think about how crazy that sounds. It is teaching a young man that loving a woman is wrong. On the other hand, Ephesians 5:25 teaches us that a man should love his woman. It says a husband should love his wife as Christ loves the church. In other words, a man should love his wife so much that he would sacrifice his life for her. In the world that I come from, a man that would die for a woman is considered soft and lame. So, while we thought that loving a girl and showing emotions was a bad thing, the Bible clearly says the opposite.

Also, look at the people who are applauded. Men who have multiple women and relationships, pimps, and players–especially in the Black community–are admired. Think about how many rappers and singers call themselves pimps in their songs. It's taboo to say you are monogamous. Loving one woman, your wife, is considered backward in the world.

Another example of the difference in the world's thinking and God's is forgiveness. If somebody does something to you in the streets, you are supposed to react quickly with anger and revenge. But the Word says a wise man is slow to anger and you are supposed to forgive and let vengeance be God's. Forgiveness is stupidity to the world. Rick Ross has an album called "God Forgives. I Don't." However, the Word literally says we should forgive. Jesus said that if someone slaps you, you must not hit him back but turn the other cheek (Matthew 5:39). We are also supposed to be generous and give. It's better to give than to receive. That's not what the world says. I can go on and on about the differences. The Word is God's way, the right way. The world says to do the opposite.

Quamé: Is this spiritual mindset conducive to surviving and thriving in the communities we grew up in? Is it reasonable to say that men in our communities need to be forgiving, sensitive and emotional?

Rodney: Forgiving, yes. Sensitive and emotional, it depends. The Word doesn't say be sensitive and emotional. It says to be forgiving, generous, and love your wife. When you do what God's Word says, He will protect you, no matter what the situation is. That's my belief. I was in jail with the wolves, the worst of the worst. Was it because of my toughness that nothing happened to me? No. In fact, I saw a lot of tough guys fold in jail. Nothing happened to me because I was living God's way and being obedient. Whenever a situation came about, I did my part and stood up but God did the rest. I had a few situations where guys tried me and I stood my ground. They looked at me and by the grace of God, they all decided to let me be. I believe God warned them they were better off not engaging in any type of battle with me; so they didn't. I believe in any circumstance, if you are obedient and do it God's way, He will make a way and protect you.

Quamé: You said you are important to a lot of people. Explain.

Rodney: God talks to us in mysterious ways. When Tottie and I got serious, we got king and queen chess piece tattoos on our hands. We have this same king/queen theme in our home. While in jail, God let me know that those roles were supposed to manifest beyond pictures or tattoos. I thought I was a king, but God let me know I wasn't acting like a king. God showed me how a king is truly supposed to conduct himself.

God puts us here to be examples of His way, but I didn't realize people were watching my example. There is a story in the Bible that talks about us being God's workmanship, created for good works (Ephesians 2:10). Scripture also says we are God's clay and He is the Potter (Isaiah 64:8). I learned that God is sculpting us by adding and removing clay, and this process can be painful to the clay. Sometimes while the clay is spinning on the pottery wheel, it loses its form and comes apart. God has to start the process over again from scratch.

In my case, God didn't throw the clay away. He said, "This is still good clay." Once the clay is done, God sets up the finished product to be used for the purpose He made it (a plate, bowl, or whatever). Some of us are so impressed with what God has made of others that we try to be them. If God made you a beautiful bowl and your friend a beautiful plate, be the best bowl you can be. Don't damage yourself by breaking off your edges to try to be a plate. I now see that I had that problem before. We all admire musicians, actors, and entertainers. But God called some of us to be teachers, pastors, authors, and nurses. So, I connected this lesson to the idea that people looked up to me and I realized I wasn't allowing myself to be used in the right way–to be a godly example.

Quamé: Responding to your claim of being arrogant, I made a comparison between you and Nas. How do you feel about this?

Rodney: First of all, any comparison to Nas is the ultimate compliment to me. With that analogy in mind, I'll say this: around the summer of 2004, I was doing good financially, and I bought my first piece of property, a condo in a nice neighborhood. A few months later, I bought a BMW. The chip on my shoulder was forming. I was the kid who had drug addict parents, was poor, and didn't have anything; therefore, I was not attractive to women. But once I got these material things, all of a sudden I was appealing.

My attitude changed because I started to see women's responses to me and that was irritating.

I treated people badly. I did many things unknowingly and I'm still learning about them. People are comfortable enough to speak out now and let me know about the things I've done. The core of me was still there though. Think about Nas after *Illmatic* and *It Was Written* when the success of those albums kicked in, and he went from Nasty Nas to Escobar. As a big Nas fan, I feel (a lot of Nas fans would agree) that Esco wasn't the best Nas. He wasn't the same lyricist who captured fans in those middle albums after *It Was Written* and before *Stillmatic*. But look what happened that probably brought another classic out of him–adversity, tribulation. His mom got sick with cancer. Jay-Z, the biggest artist in the game, came out publicly and attacked him. With his back against the wall and after being humbled, his next album, *Stillmatic*, is a classic. It is also my favorite album of his and one of my favorite albums of all time. Period. He also got up off the canvas and

Me at the Nas "Life Is Good Tour" concert

knocked out the champ, Jay-Z with "Either"! I also don't think it was a coincidence that the man who calls himself "God's Son" beat the man who calls himself the god MC "Jay-Hova."

Quamé: You said you learned that you owed a lot of people apologies. How did that happen?

Rodney: I'm amazed at how much God taught me in jail. In jail, during Bible study, I learned many stories that related to mine. It was mind blowing. I had already heard many of these stories at church, but I never equated them to my life or anybody's life that I knew. But that's what a humbling situation does. It opens your mind and heart. I didn't realize until I was in jail that Satan's fall was due to arrogance. Pride comes before a fall. (Proverbs 16:18)

Now, the message is "Check yourself before God has to do it for you." I learned to lead with humility and that apologizing is not being weak. Actually, it is being strong. I learned from my ex-wife that I can't worry about the response to my apology; I just have to do my part. A person may not be in the place to receive it or to articulate an acceptance of it. But apologizing is liberating for the person who is doing it. One person I want to apologize to for the poor example I set is my cousin, Walt. I was the first person to put a gun in his hand. I made carrying pistols look cool. He has since had a gun charge. I feel somewhat responsible for whatever missteps he made because of my actions and example.

Quamé: How did you arrive at those epiphanies you had in jail? Can you give some detailed examples?

Rodney: I started to pray and call out to God for His deliverance from the situation when I was in 2400. But I received no answer– at least, so I thought. I thought His answer would come in a dismissal of the case, a bail reduction, or something like that. I went to court, twice, for a bail reduction and for the court to drop the charges from 2nd-degree murder to manslaughter as they should have been from the start. No love! Both denied. So, I was heartbroken. I was asking God to show me a sign He cares and still hears me. That's when I got called to be moved to 5200. And, the first thing I saw on that floor was the chapel. I immediately started going to church services and Bible studies. God began to change me from the inside out. I learned the way He does that is through His Word. Slowly but surely, I saw changes in my court situation. It went from no offers to twelve years at 80 percent, to ten years at 80 percent, to ten years at 50 percent. Also, a law had just been passed called "Proposition 57." Proposition 57 reduced sentences of non-violent offenders like me from having to serve 50 percent of their prison time to 33 percent. The epiphanies were all a part of the learning, acceptance, and then restoration.

Quamé: Prior to your accident and going to jail, what do you think your biggest fear was?

Rodney: Going to jail for a long time was my biggest fear. I remember saying that to somebody before. I took a poetry class in the pen. In one of my poems, I said, "When God wants to get your attention, sometimes He uses your greatest fear." That is exactly what He did to me.

Quamé: How did jail become one of your biggest fears? Can you recall when that fear was evident to you? How old were you?

Rodney: When I was around 21 years old, I went to jail for possession of a loaded concealed firearm. The gun was registered to me, so the jail stay was only overnight. However, being locked in a cell overnight was enough to let me know it wasn't anything I ever wanted to do again. I am a person who hates to waste time because I am wired to constantly be productive. Sitting in a jail cell doing nothing is the opposite of that. It is the worst thing you can do to somebody like me. Being in that position for a long time was torture. I realized that that night.

North Kern State Prison (Delano, CA)

Quamé: Do you miss basketball? What is your relationship like with basketball today? Do your injuries from your accident prevent you from playing and/or have you considered coaching?

Rodney: Yes, I do miss basketball very much. Basketball is in my blood. I've been playing since I was five years old. It came naturally to me. When I woke up from the accident, and they explained how serious my injuries were, the first question that popped into my mind was, "Will I be able to play basketball again, and if so, will I be anywhere close to what I used to be?" That's how much I love basketball.

When I was arrested and sent to MCJ, I was limping around for a long time because my tibia was still slightly broken. After being moved to the school dorm, one of the young dudes noticed the basketball tattoo on my calf. He asked me if I was one of those dudes who got basketball tattoos but really couldn't hoop. He was basically calling me out. He asked me to go to the yard one Sunday morning on the roof of MCJ. After a bit of clowning and calling me out, I agreed.

That Sunday, I realized how much I had damaged my tibia. It was about ten months since the accident, but I was nowhere near normal. I remember getting the ball, and the same person who was calling me out was guarding me. I did my go-to move, a right-to-left crossover between the back of my legs. He went for the ball and I went around him. Everybody out there was ooohing and ahhing, but when it was time to jump to make the lay-up, I had no lift. I felt a sharp pain near my left ankle. After that, I was hobbling on the court at times. I was favoring my left leg, which was crazy. I was still good enough to show everybody I had game, but I was disappointed because I wasn't sure if I would ever be anywhere near my old self. In the shower when we got back to the dorm, I shed a couple of tears. That's how hurt I was.

I continued to play here and there in the county but being a shell of my former self wore on me. I stopped after a while because I was so hurt, and there was not enough room on their makeshift half basketball/racketball court. Plus, the court was covered by a thick mesh that was so low, you couldn't put any arch on your jump shot because you would hit the covering. It was wack.

Tottie and me in the visiting room at North Kern Prison – 2020

When I got to the pen twenty months later, the first thing I saw when I got to the yard was the basketball court. It was better than the one at the county. It was an official-size full court with nets and everything. I hadn't played in like six months, and I didn't want to because of how I felt the last time. So I started to walk the track twice a day. After a month, I started to walk and jog. Then I started running the track. God was answering my prayers and healing me. Months after I arrived there, I got on the court. I was a lot better, but I was still favoring my tibia a little. Running fast and jumping were cool, but lateral movements were a problem.

Still being the cocky, arrogant kid from the Inglewood YMCA, I found myself getting into little arguments on the court. Not wanting to get into any fights in the pen and possibly add to my time, I stopped playing basketball during my last couple of months there. But because I had shown people I had game and word got around I played a little college ball, I was elected the coordinator of the yard's basketball tournament. What's funny about that is I wasn't there when I was elected, and I did not want to do it.

Once I saw how many people were pushing for me to be involved, I agreed. I drew up real tournament brackets and refereed the whole tournament. It's funny how a small thing like a basketball tournament can boost people's spirits. People were talking about the tournament for weeks after. Even the guards were watching the games.

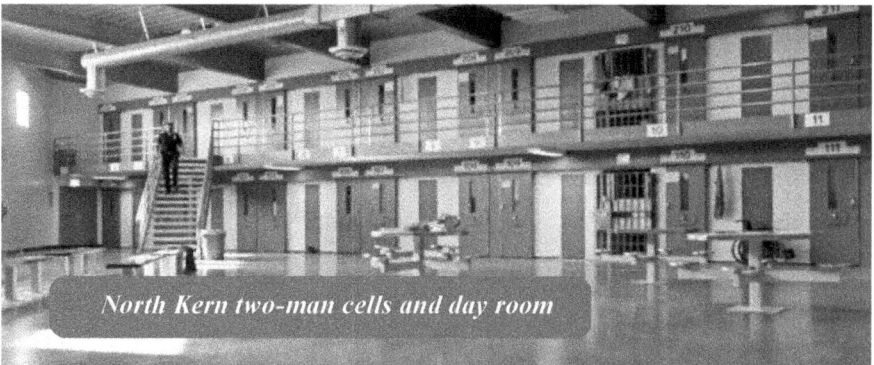
North Kern two-man cells and day room

Throughout the Bible, it talks about God giving His children favor wherever they are. The book of Genesis talks about Joseph in prison.

> But the Lord was with Joseph and showed him mercy, and He gave him favor in the sight of the keeper of the prison. (Genesis 39:21)

Being imprisoned was by far the worst time of my life. However, I can say God was with me and gave me favor in the eyes of a lot of people. For sure! Anyway, I was moved to the halfway house in Long Beach. They had a half court there. They also had some young dudes who could really play. Again, they managed to see my tattoo and asked me to come to play. After some persuading, I did.

When I got out there, I didn't take long at all to see I was pretty much completely healed. My lateral movements were good. No pain. I was able to cross-over just like before. That night, while alone, I cried tears of joy because I knew God had answered my prayers from that first night

Kennedy, me, and Emory – Christmas Day 2021 (Daddy Elf dress-up)

in the hospital over three years before. They even had a 3-on-3 tournament I played in and made it to the finals. All that to say, I can still hoop. The only difference is what Father Time has done, which was going to happen with or without the accident.

I want to coach youth basketball. I ran into my boy who used to play in the same AAU traveling leagues I used to play in. We are talking about possibly starting a youth team.

Quamé: You called yourself "spiritual." What does that mean to you? Can you share some of your beliefs that you feel make you "spiritual"?

Rodney: Being spiritual is having a personal relationship with God. It is being able to talk to God and expect a response however He sends it. Religion is the study of God or many gods. God is our Father in heaven. If you look at God as your Father who loves you as a father should, you are more likely to be spiritual. I believe those who see religion as something you learn to do and God as just a

Me and my daughters (left to right) De'jah, Lyric, Me, Emory, and Kennedy – 2017

higher power who judges and condemns us for the things we do wrong are religious, not spiritual. Jesus was trying to show people how to be spiritual. The Pharisees, who were the religious leaders of Jesus' day, were representative of religious people. They thought they were spiritual because they went to the synagogue and knew the Scriptures more than the average person, but they lacked the relationship, which is the most important part.

Quamé: What's your biggest concern currently as a parent?

Rodney: My biggest concern is that I won't be able to have the protective, fatherly relationship with my girls that I think every daughter should have because of the choices I've made. I am a very hands-on father. The worst part about being in prison was not seeing my daughters and being unable to provide the teachings, discipline, and protection I am used to giving.

I had to hear about De'jah graduating from college in a letter. This is a day I dreamed about since she was born; I missed that. There's a scar on my heart because I missed that day. She also did not graduate from Baylor, the school she was attending when I was out because, I believe, I wasn't able to pay my portion of her tuition. Therefore, she had to transfer to UT Austin, a cheaper school, where she graduated from.

Lyric and I are not as close as we used to be because I was gone and her mother and I don't talk. Kennedy and I are trying to build a relationship, but because she was conceived while I was in a relationship with Tottie, Emory's mom, that makes the situation very touchy. Emory and I are very close. She is the only child who lives with me.

It's hard and a constant struggle. I never thought my relationship with my daughters would be like this, but it is. I love them with all my heart, but due to issues with their mothers, mostly caused by me, I admit, we're not as close as we were or as close as I wish. That hurts, but I believe God will repair it all in time.

SECTION 4

PURPOSE AND NEW OUTLOOK ON LIFE

THE PROMISED LAND

CHAPTER 16

RE-ENTRY AND THE SYSTEM

Quamé: What was your release date from the halfway house?

Rodney: I was released on July 31st, 2020. Currently, I'm on parole. I was given a ten-year sentence and required to serve 50 percent of that, which is five years. I served three years in jail and the remaining two are to be served at home. I can get off early for good behavior. In March of 2020, I was sent from the actual prison yard to the halfway house or what they call MCRP – Men's Community Reentry Program

MCRP and halfway houses are places they should have for everybody being released from prison. There are only three of them in the county of Los Angeles. Very few of them are in the state, and you must be very lucky and privileged to get accepted. I was accepted because God blessed me with that.

MCRP Long Beach facility

We need more programs like those, especially for people who have been gone for a long time. The norm is they release you and no matter how long you've been gone (you could have been gone for twenty years), they give you $200 and put you on the street. They make you buy a bus ticket with some of that money to get wherever you're going. Let's just say your bus ticket is $60; you have $140 left to start your life. And they just say, "Go."

The re-entry program allows you to serve the last year-and-a-half of your sentence at a facility in the city where they teach you job skills and allow you to go out and work. However, you wear an ankle monitor that tracks you 24 hours a day. You must return to the facility in the evening. You get three good meals a day and a place to sleep while you are transitioning back into society. They make you save the majority of your work checks, so when you're fully released, you have savings to go rent an apartment or whatever, instead of them just giving you $200 and saying figure it out.

Me at the MCRP facility wearing an ankle monitor – 2020

They came up with programs like that to decrease recidivism–which at the time was 65 percent. Meaning 65 percent of the people who were released from prison ended up going back. More programs like these are needed to reduce recidivism, but the politics of it stands in the way. We need to understand that locking people up is not the only way to help society.

Without these programs, you are putting worse criminals back out in the community. Even if someone wants to change, how will $140 help them with a new start in their lives when you put them out on the streets? What are they supposed to do with $140?

A lot of them return to criminal activity to simply survive and they're right back in jail. I want to help lower recidivism. More funding is needed for these programs. People leaving prison should have a place to go. We should give people a head start. In the long run, the community will be safer without a bunch of ex-felons there trying to figure it out, returning to criminal activity, and going back to jail where taxpayers feed and house them.

Quamé: It sounds like a no-brainer. Why do you think they don't have more programs like that, and why aren't they doing this?

Rodney: A lot of citizens/people don't look at it from an economic standpoint. First of all, they figure, "Hey, just lock these people up. They committed crimes so lock them up and forget about them." They do not think about the tax money that is used for them to eat and be housed. Police officers and correctional officers are the main ones who do not want programs like this to exist because they don't want the prison population to be reduced. Some of the prisons would have to close down if fewer people commit crimes and go back to jail. People like district attorneys and parole officers also don't want that. I didn't realize this before, but there's a whole lot of money in the prison system. They also have several private prisons that make a ton of money.

Federal money goes to the county for the prisoners. They house us like cattle and the system is a bunch of nonsense. They have to pay for the buses and officers who take us to court for five minutes. In court, they ask, "Are you guys ready?"

Your counsel responds, "No, we need another month for whatever."

They respond, "Okay, we'll see you in another month, Mr. Wright."

Then they schedule another court date. I did that fifteen times! Why not be more efficient and get the job done in a shorter timeframe? They don't want that because everyone is getting paid in this process—the court typists, the attorneys, judges, the court officers, the bus drivers; it's a big industry. Our situations are paying everybody. It's all about money rather than efficiency and compassion. What's going on?

I was ready for my case for at least six months. But the response was, "Okay, we're going to do some more talking and then come back." In my opinion, it could be handled in a few conversations but not enough people would get paid if it takes a few days, not years.

CHAPTER 17

THE FIRST YEAR OUT OF PRISON

Quamé: When you were released on July 31, 2020, what was one of the first things you did once you got home? Since that time, what wave have you been on? What's life been like for you?

Rodney: The first thing I did was get a real haircut because that's just me (laughing). I'm just like that. I have to be presentable. In jail, they don't have clippers or anything like that to cut hair, so barbers do it with disposable razors positioned in small combs. Some barbers are talented and can cut very well with razors, but they are rare. I went straight to Inglewood to see Nonnie and Kennedy. When you're in prison serving time, you dream of the day of your release. You talk about it more and more as the day approaches: "What's the first thing you're going to do?" In my entire life, I have never experienced a feeling like the one I had when I was released.

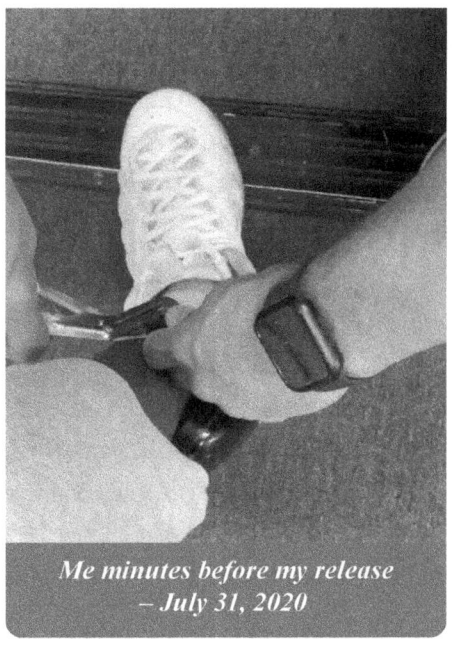

Me minutes before my release – July 31, 2020

First of all, I was released early due to COVID-19. By that time, I had gotten my release date down to December 2020. They announced on the news that they were releasing people early. They posted lists on the board and said they were releasing people up to six months early. I only had three or four months left. But some people had the full six months left, and their names hit the list to get out before mine. When I talked to the directors about it, they would say, "Hey, Sacramento is in charge of this. There's no rhyme or reason of the order they are releasing people. It's not in alphabetical order or in accordance with the crimes committed. When your name pops up and they give you the early release date in the system, we put it up on the board." I went through that for a month or so.

I saw many people whose release dates were well after mine packing up, leaving, and slapping high-fives on their way out. Finally, my name went up on the board for August 13th, which was a month away at the time. Everything was up in the air, and I didn't know what was going to happen. On a side note, some people were supposed to get out, but their releases were rescinded because they had "holds" or warrants they didn't know about. This meant they would be sent back to the county jail to go to court for the hold and do the entire process over again. All of that was going through my head. "Man, I hope I don't have any holds or anything like that," I would say.

Ironically, they pushed my release date up again to that same week. I was happy but also still in disbelief. I couldn't believe that this long, life-changing process was coming to an end. I didn't believe it until they finally cut the ankle monitor off my ankle and I walked out that door. It was the happiest I've ever been in my life! The feeling is unexplainable. I can't even put it into words. It's up there with the birth of my children and when I took my daughter to college and checked her into her dorm.

The other part of your question was "What wave have I been on?"

Quamé: Wait! Hold on, before you get there, you just said something so deep that it took me a second to register. You said when you were released, it was one of the happiest days of your life. You compared it to the birth of your daughters and dropping your eldest daughter off on her first day of college. Isn't that crazy how going through something so horrific resulted in a feeling that's equated with some of the greatest things anyone can experience in life? That's deep to me!

Rodney: Yeah, yeah. Aye man, with what just happened with DMX passing, I've been you know…

Quamé: I'm a huge DMX fan!

Rodney: Me too man. I am not just a fan of his music but also of him as a person. Most artists can't say that. A lot of my favorite rappers are not as good as he was as a person. You know what I'm saying. He had both qualities.

Very few people have the honest, true spirit that connects with people, and the musical talent to articulate it. He was one of them. Very few like him come along in a lifetime–Nipsey Hussle, Tupac. While DMX was in a coma,

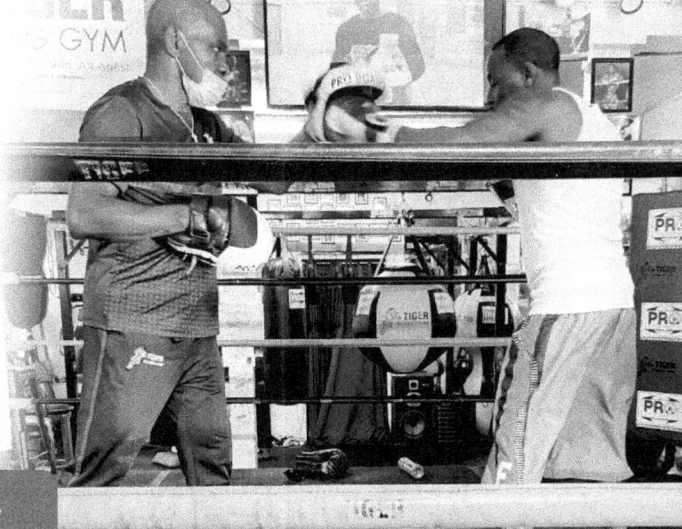

Me returning to boxing training – October 2020

I was listening to a lot of his music and watching his videos and interviews. He made a comment just similar to what you said, and I'm paraphrasing, "The biggest struggles birth the biggest breakthroughs." That's what that was. I'll never forget that day. It was unexplainable. When I walked out of there and pulled off in a car, I breathed a sigh of relief, "Wheew man, it's finally over!" I have footage of it all!

Quamé: Who picked you up?

Rodney: It's funny because since my date got pushed up I was trying to surprise everybody. Tottie was out of town in Fresno for a funeral, so I didn't tell her. She knew about the August 13th date, but she didn't know they had moved it up again. She told me, "I'm gonna go to the funeral and I'll be back some time that night." So, I

Lyric, me, and Emory – July 4, 2021

decided I would go home and when she returned from the funeral, she would be surprised to see me there. However, when she got to Fresno, she said she wanted to stay some extra days. Kryme, my cousin Alluron, and my boy Marlon whom I had met when I was in the county picked me up.

Quamé: Oh, Marlon was released already. Why was he in jail?

Rodney: Yeah, he was released a year before. Now, he is a photographer and a videographer. He was convicted for having stolen equipment or something like that, nothing too crazy.

Marlon asked me if I wanted to shoot some footage of my first day out. So, we got a lot of footage of that day. Bro, it's like you said: something so horrific and life-changing birthed that moment.

I talked to my boy who I met in jail and who was on his 3rd prison stint, and he told me it will take about a year to a year-and-a-half to settle back into normalcy. That helped me a lot because I thought that once I was released I would just hit the ground running and never look back.

> As for you also, Because of the blood of your covenant, I will set your prisoners free from the waterless pit. Return to the stronghold, You prisoners of hope. Even today I declare ThatI will restore double to you. (Zechariah 9:11-12)

I've been standing on that promise of restoration, but I think I was expecting immediate restoration. So, when he said it usually takes a year or so to settle back in, that helped me to relax a little.

Quamé: How long have you been out now?

Rodney: It's been eight months and some change. It's a struggle and an adjustment.

Quamé: What's the biggest adjustment you have had to make?

Rodney: Getting back on my feet financially without making money as big a priority as it was before. That's what first comes to my mind because of who I was compared to the new me. I'm not the same. When I got out, I realized everybody was expecting the same, and everybody was the same. They are who they were three years ago, and I'm a totally different person. So, all of the people around me, especially the close people are expecting the same me. They have to get used to a different me. There has to be an adjustment and that's a process.

Quamé: In what ways are you most different?

Rodney: I think in everything. My approach to life and my outlook are different.

Tottie, Emory, Kennedy, me, and Zailenn – Christmas Day 2020

Q uamé: Let's start right there. What's your new outlook?

Rodney: I'm a lot more compassionate. When you've received so much grace and forgiveness for the things you've done, you can't help but to have that for other people. And sometimes, even that's a struggle because where we're from, being compassionate can come across as soft. It gives you a lot of patience. I think that's the answer, patience. You can't help but have patience when you are forced to have patience. When you want to hurry something up to whatever it's going to be, and the people are sitting back playing, making you wait because of the bureaucracy and how everything is set up, you become patient. So, I have a lot more patience, compassion, and grace.

I'm not trying to sign up for the rat race again. That's what everybody is doing. Another big change for me is I'm not as concerned with monetary gain as much as I was before. It's still there somewhat because in this life you have to make money to survive and live. But it isn't as important as it was. God provided for me while I was gone. I didn't lose much at all. The funny thing is I thought everything was going to be gone!

In the county, everything costs four times the amount it does on the street. So, they're bleeding you dry just to survive. To eat something halfway decent will cost you four or five times more than what it costs on the street. Think about it; you're in there and you're not making money, but regular food and hygiene cost you so much. You can easily go broke. Most people do, and then you're dependent on other people. I know God provided because different doors just opened up. What people said wouldn't happen, happened. My lawyer said, "They're probably going to take your house where you live and definitely your income property." But no, I was able to sell my income property. I paid two lawyers and still had money left. I survived in jail for three years lacking nothing.

I didn't know how Tottie was going to keep our house where we lived. Logically, there was no way she could afford it. I was paying 75% of the bills and I was working a lot of overtime to do that. God opened up doors. We got something in the mail that said, "Hey, we can do a modification." It was a 50/50 chance whether it would get approved or not, but, of course, God blessed us, and she got approved. God adjusted the mortgage payment to fit her income for five years. Nothing was taken despite the lawyer saying, "They are going to take this. They're going to take that." I had a 401k I had been saving since I was twenty-one and the lawyer said, "That's gone." Nope. They ended up cashing me out for that while I was in prison.

While in prison I got the revelation I was going through the wilderness process. If you're not familiar with the story in Exodus, check it out. When God's people were in Egypt in bondage, He delivered them. You know the story about the parting of the Red Sea. Here's the correlation. When in bondage, you get used to it.

The Israelites walked through the Red Sea and they got to the other side. Now, their goal was to reach the Promised Land, which was a three-week trip through the wilderness. But it took them forty years because God sent them around the mountain. He did this because they had been in bondage so long, they were used to doing things the way the Egyptians did. Egypt represents the world, society in general.

When God says He will deliver you and take you out of bondage, there's always a wilderness time. Because when you get to the Promised Land, He will not allow what you learned in society (Egypt) there. There is always a wilderness process. After you've been delivered and you're out of bondage, it takes time to release all of the things you learned while you were in bondage.

In the wilderness, God provides for you. The Israelites were surrounded by desert and wondered how they were going to eat because they couldn't farm in the desert. God sent down manna (a sweet-tasting food) from heaven and the people ate. Then God gave them quails. It rained food. That's what happened while I was in jail. God supernaturally provided for me and my family. How does an entire family manage a mortgage and my food allowance of $100 a week, without my bulk of the household earnings? How did we keep everything? That's a miracle! Not to mention, they charge a ridiculous amount for inmates to talk on the phone, and I talked on the phone every night for hours sometimes. So, I was a large bill every month.

The horrible conditions are set up this way because they want you to take the first deal they throw at you, which is always a bad deal. My wife had to come to the jail to put money on the books every week. Imagine, I was earning over $100,000 a year, and my wife maybe $35,000. We had a high house note and car notes. I was working overtime to maintain this lifestyle, and suddenly the bulk of that money is taken away. Add me, the main earner, as a bill, not a contributor. I thought there was no way possible it was sustainable. Actually, it was illogical for that to happen. But that's the definition of a miracle. It was revealed to me that when you're in the wilderness, God will provide.

I was in bondage before the accident and my survival was a miracle (similar to the Red Sea parting). The miracle represented the start of the process of God taking me to the Promised Land. The next part was the wilderness. God was not going to allow anything I learned in The Bottoms or wherever into the Promised Land. I learned that the Promised Land is you walking in your purpose. When you walk in whatever God put you on the earth to do, that's your Promised Land.

The jail was part of my wilderness and God provided for me there. The wilderness isn't easy. You can't provide for yourself there just as the Israelites couldn't in the desert. However, when you read the story, the wilderness was necessary because whenever the people met an obstacle, they always wanted to revert to what they learned in Egypt. For example, when Moses went up the mountain to get the commandments from God, he was gone for forty days. In that forty day period, the people thought Moses had died. They lost hope because they thought their leader was gone and God had left them. So, they made a golden calf for themselves to worship. They learned the idolatrous practices in Egypt. Every time they faced an obstacle and doubt arose, they wanted to go back to Egypt and slavery.

When people get out of jail and they're faced with an obstacle like the need for money, many revert to what they learned in their environment (Egypt). I would be lying if I didn't say it hadn't at least crossed my mind. I'm Automatik, PJ's nephew. I know how to hustle up some money. But, I have to remind myself that God will provide. I may not see it right now, but He will surely provide. That's faith. That's the definition of faith, knowing that something is there, even though you don't see it. It isn't easy, especially when everyone around you is asking, "Where is the money going to come from?"

> Now faith is the substance of things hoped for, the evidence of things not seen. (Hebrews 11:1)

When the people around you don't have that same faith, it makes the issue that much harder. It's a struggle.

Quamé: Some of the main differences you note about yourself are that you're more compassionate and you have more patience and faith. What are some of the everyday actions that you weren't doing before, which reflect this new mindset?

Rodney: I am way more focused on peace, inner peace. I'm learning to appreciate the simple stuff. For the twenty months in the county, I wasn't able to walk past thirty feet in the dorm or five feet in the cells. Every day, I could only look at stone walls, and I was not allowed to go outside at all. So, when I got to the prison yard twenty-three months later, I was super relieved and thankful. It was amazing just to walk up and see the basketball courts and the track... something so simple. I will never take that for granted again. Now, I walk daily. I go to the beach and ride bikes. The second-best day I've had since I've been out is the day my family and I went to the beach and rode bikes.

When you're put in a position I was in–and you don't know if you will ever see the ocean again–you dream about doing that type of stuff. I realized that I was stuck in the rat race, chasing money and material things, which don't bring you peace or happiness. I told myself one of the first things I was going to do when I got out was go to the beach. I lived in Los Angeles all this time, and Inglewood is ten minutes from the beach, but I seldom went. I met people there from other states who said, "Man, I know you go to the beach all the time." All I could say was, "No, not really." That's one of the many things those of us in LA take for granted. Even though I said one of the first things I was going to do when I got out was going to the beach, I didn't make it. I just went about three weeks ago. It was so peaceful. I was just riding. The next thing I knew, two hours had gone by, and we had to get the rented bikes back.

Quamé: Which beach did you go to?

Rodney: We went to Manhattan Beach. We just got on the bikes and rode south. We were in Torrance going toward Palos Verdes. It was so peaceful. I'm incorporating that kind of stuff into my life.

Peace is the most important thing. I had a little money and so-called accomplishments before, but I didn't have peace. You can "trick off" your financial accomplishments by not having peace. That's why you see millionaires commit suicide. They don't have inner peace. Their lives and priorities are out of order. God put my life, priorities, and perspective in order while I was in jail.

Quamé: Peace became your foundation. You had the roof, but you were missing the foundation.

Rodney: Exactly. Without the foundation of Jesus, everything will collapse. Now, it's in proper order. My life was all out of wack. Now, I know the proper order. You must put God first because peace comes from Him. Before, the order was my daughters, finances, then finances again, Nonnie, God, my cars, etc. I thought that was the right way because that is the way of the world I came from. But now I learned that was a life lived out of order. That's why I was not happy.

Family is up there but after God. Family is before finances. I had my family structure out of wack too. Maybe none of my relationships worked because my daughters were number one. People in the world would hear me say my daughters came first in my life and applaud. But once you learn God's order–your wife is number one. People who know me will say, "Aww, yeah, he has changed a lot." My mindset was that no woman was going to come before my kids. But that's not the proper order. The funny thing is that Nicole's father, who is a pastor, told me that when I was much younger, but I wasn't ready to receive it at the time. He had a good explanation too. He said the kids would get to a certain age and leave and then I'd be secondary to them. So, you can't place your kids above the person who will still be there with you, your wife. I thought he was just saying that because he wanted his daughter to be first in my life. But he was right. I know the order now–wife, children, and then extended family.

God fixed everything while I was in jail. It took the whole three years to change me. You would think the accident and the trauma from it would change me, but no. I know now that I would have gone right back to the same way I was before the accident, back to the rat race. The wilderness time was necessary.

CHAPTER 18

PEACE IS THE GREATEST ACCOMPLISHMENT

Quamé: We're in the last chapter of the book. Where do we go from here? What are you looking forward to? Since you have a new outlook on life, what do you foresee this outlook will bring? A new outlook means a new reality. So what do you think this new reality will be moving forward–good or bad?

Rodney: This is what I know, bro. I can't help but be a lot better because my focus is God and peace. And guess what? Anything can go that takes away from my peace. The scary part is you never know what or who that's going to be. That's the hard part. Every day, I learn that God may be removing some of the closest people to me because they are still on that old stuff. They're trying to pull me back, and I'm trying to show them what I've learned and bring them over to this side, but it's a tug of war. It's not easy because these are good people at heart. Here's an example. If you're an ex-drug dealer and you go to jail, while you're in jail, your drug dealing crew takes care of you. When you get out and tell them you're not selling drugs anymore, they will say, "That's good, bro, good luck." When the struggles hit, you need people around you to hold you accountable and not let you sell drugs when you get weak. You can't have people around who offer you drugs to sell. You have to get away from those people. That's the struggle.

I see a lot of that around; I see it all. My goal is not what it was before. I was trying to accumulate a bunch of material things, thinking that possessions would make me happy. Now, I'm trying to downsize, because things can keep you in bondage. I see people who want to spend a million dollars on a house they can't afford. They get the house and then have to work hard for the next thirty years just to scrape by. It's all to show someone else how nice your house is. I'm not doing that anymore.

I was working six to seven days a week. I was averaging sixty-plus hours a week, sometimes eighty, just to sustain that mess. I'm not trying to do that anymore. But this new mindset doesn't make sense to a lot of people around me. As I said, I'm at peace when I'm out there riding a bike. Before, there was no way I could be at peace at the beach unless I was driving a Bentley or something down Pacific Coast Highway. I don't look at it the same way anymore.

I let God show me and, at the same time, He gives me free will. God may show me a certain person has to go. When you know he's a good person and you care about him, it's very difficult. But, I can't let anyone come between me and my peace. Everything can go.

Quamé: Wow! I needed to hear that last line, "Everything can go."

Rodney: Aww, man if it's coming between you and your peace, it has to go.

Quamé: That is deep. Hey, you're on another level!

Rodney: Yeah, and you understand it because you're there too. Most people I know are not. They would say the same statement you said, but they would look at it differently.

Quamé: I know what you mean!

Rodney: They would say, "Um, he is on another new level (like a lower level)." And I'm thinking yeah, yeah it may look like a lower level to you, but it's definitely higher.

Quamé: They think you're a hippie or something.

Rodney: I guess so. But I don't care. Think about this; I have never in my life ridden a bike on the beach. Being from LA that's a shame. There weren't too many of us out there doing it either.

Quamé: That's crazy.

Rodney: I don't think we saw another Black person out there riding bikes at all.

Quamé: Yeah, let me ask you something and this will probably be my last question. You answered in-depth and well where you are now. That last statement, that's what I see too. Whenever I do stuff, whether it's camping, getting an RV, being on the beach, doing anything with nature, going to certain restaurants where they don't serve meat, I don't see my people. Why not? What's your theory as to why we look at things like that with disdain? When they see us doing these things, they think we are weirdos; we're acting White; we're not the same, or whatever they say. Why do you think Black people judge one another in that way?

Rodney: I think most of us buy or have bought into what I was just talking about. We usually don't come from affluent families, so the whole purpose in life becomes getting money. Then once you get it, get more. Somehow, we have bought into the lie that having money and material things equates to happiness and peace. But it doesn't. So when you're out there doing something peaceful, they want to know why you are not out there making money. The idea is you don't have the time to be riding bikes at the beach. You should be grinding every hour of the day. I bought that lie. I had all of that and was depressed. That's what is put into our minds since we are young.

It has been fed to us in our music and the environment we're from. We are taught to grind, get money, flaunt it, spend it frivolously, and get more; get more, and get more. Where's the peace? Where's the freedom? Dress like this, look like this.

I was having a conversation the other day, and my boy and I both agreed that one of the freest people in the music industry is Andre 3000. He's not in any box of how to dress or what he should rap about. Look at the person he was when Outkast first came out. He was the prototypical image of a southern rapper, and it worked! Then on the next album *ATaliens*, you could see the progression; he was changing. What's the first thing everybody thought about him? He's a weirdo. It took me a while because, at first, I thought that too. I wondered what he was doing. I liked the Andre from *Southernplayalisticadillacmuzik* with the Kango hat on and driving the Cadillac! He said, "I'm in search of freedom, something that none of y'all have. I'm not going to let y'all keep me in a box when it comes to my artistic expression."

What I realize now is he got way doper when he allowed himself to be free. His mind was able to expand, and he wasn't in the box we, the record label, or society tried to put him in. He said he was trying to be a true artist and would wear whatever he wanted to wear. He became one of the best to ever do it. I think that happened because he wasn't locked in a box. That's where I'm trying to get to. I'm not there yet, but I wish I was that free to wear cowboy boots and a cummerbund with no shirt. I'm not saying I will do that, but what I can say is I will do what makes me feel at peace. Someone might say, "Man, Auto is out there riding bikes and going camping like a White boy."

If I'm at peace, I don't care what people say. When I was doing what they thought was praiseworthy I was not happy. I was depressed and trying to find happiness and peace. It was nowhere to be found. It wasn't in going out to clubs all the time. It wasn't in drinking. It wasn't in pills or sleeping with a bunch of women. It was as simple as going to the beach and looking at nature and the things God provides. It's a relationship with God and confirming it by going

Lyric, Tottie, me, Emory, and De'jah on a gamily bike riding day in Manhattan Beach, CA the Summer of 2021

to look at the natural things He gave us. God is saying, "You're out here running around chasing something that I pretty much gave you for free. You're buying into the lies the Enemy sold you. You're trying to provide when I have already provided everything you need." God had to sit me down in a hospital and a prison and put me in a place where I couldn't provide for myself to show me: "I [God] can provide for you. You thought that you went and got that job." "I [God] got you that job." I had to sit back and think about how that job (at the gas company) came about. It was a 100 percent blessing! Real talk.

I kept getting promoted over the years. But when I forgot that and thought I did it, God took it because I didn't appreciate it. That's what the Word says in so many of the stories in the Bible. God picks us to do something but many times we get arrogant. God sends little signs that say, "Hey, you're getting arrogant; bring it back. Understand *I* gave this to you." But we get out there and arrogantly think, "I did all this." Then God says, "Enough is enough, but I'm [God] not going to kill you [referring to my situation]. I'm just going to show you and teach you. I'm going to restore all of those things to you and more but let Me take them temporarily because you're worshiping the blessings, not the Blesser.

Quamé: What, you're dropping it!

Rodney: I can't take credit for any of this. It's just the experiences and what I've learned speaking. God did it. God could've removed me.

Imagine coming back from that and knowing all of that, it's a great feeling. It's also a disappointment because I came back to the people who haven't been through anything, and they're all the same. I'm looking at them and I'm trying to warn them about worshiping the blessings. They think something is wrong with me. They act as if they hear me but then they go right back to chasing the blessings.

Quamé: Do you think that "rock bottoms" are absolutely necessary for people to change?

Rodney: It's true for a lot of people but not everybody. There's a saying that a wise person can learn from wise counsel. A stupid person has to go through to learn their lesson. If you're walking down the street and a person a few yards in front of you falls into a hole in the ground. When the person climbs out of the hole and says, "Hey, watch out for that hole! Don't fall in it," a wise person says, "Okay, I appreciate that" and avoids that pitfall. A dumb person says, "Man, I know what I'm doing. I'm not going to fall in it like you," and then boom, falls into the hole. That's an arrogant and stubborn person. The Bible calls it a "hardened heart." There are a lot of hardened hearts out here around me. I know for sure I was one of them because people couldn't tell me much before either.

You don't have to go through what I did. I hope that's what people get out of this book. Learn from my mistakes and anybody else's, so you don't have to go through your own head-on collision. You don't have to go through your own wilderness; just listen and learn. Listen to somebody else's testimony about the pitfalls and avoid them. But when you're stubborn, pitfalls are necessary. I guess I was that stubborn.

Quamé: That's a powerful note to end on. Do you have any final words?

Rodney: I understand the struggle; this walk through life is not easy. It is not easy to do a complete 180-degree turn from everything you've been taught. It's a struggle every day and you will not have it all together. You will make mistakes, but don't let them deter you. That's the hard part.

> For a righteous man may fall seven times and
> rise again. (Proverbs 24:16a)

I will fall and make mistakes, even on this side of the wilderness. But I know my priorities are in order at this point. I am seeking the things I didn't think I needed like peace and love. I had given up on love. I didn't even think there was real love in this world. I know love and peace are very important now. You can't live a happy life without them. They are at the top of my priority list. Finances and possessions will come. God will provide them. I have seen Him provide out of nothing. He made a way where there seemed to be none, a way through the wilderness.

Money shouldn't be your god. Jesus said to seek first the kingdom of God:

> So do not worry, saying, 'What shall we eat?' or 'What shall we drink?' or 'What shall we wear?' For the pagans run after all these things, and your heavenly Father knows that you need them. But seek first his kingdom and his righteousness, and all these things will be given to you as well. Therefore do not worry about tomorrow, for tomorrow will worry about itself. Each day has enough trouble of its own. (Matthew 6:31-34 NIV).

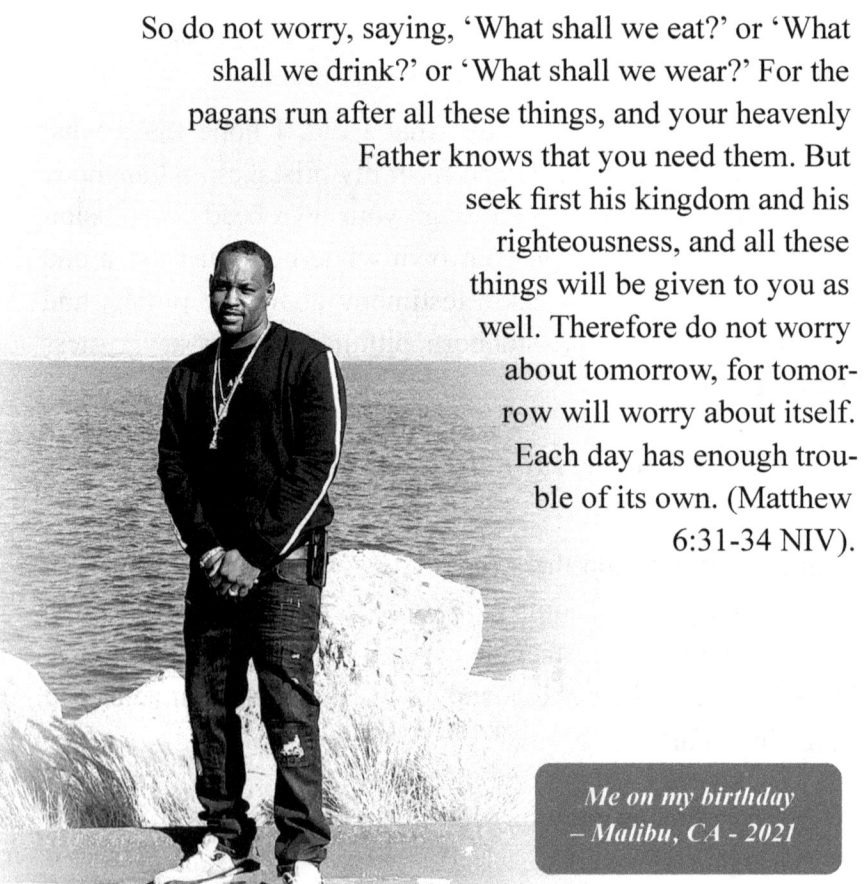

Me on my birthday – Malibu, CA - 2021

God is saying, "Chase Me, and I will give you all of that stuff in abundance." As I said, it's not easy, especially when all you know is to chase money and things. I'm chasing peace and happiness now; that's what I'm chasing. Millionaires pay thousands upon thousands of dollars to therapists trying to find peace and happiness.

I get it now, but I didn't get it before. I used to think, "They have money; why are they so unhappy?" Now, I get it. The worst time in my life was when I had the most monetarily. I'll never forget that. So anything and anybody trying to come in between me and my peace can go. If I end up on the beach in an RV, I'll be happy. I guarantee that everybody who knows me will say, "Auto went nuts! He's got an RV living on the beach with a bike! He has lost his mind!" But when they visit me, I guarantee they will also say, "I've never seen him so happy though!"

This is my prayer for you:

The Lord bless you and keep you; the Lord make his face shine on you and be gracious to you; the Lord turn his face toward you and give you peace.
(Numbers 6:24-26)

Me in front of the remains of my truck

Epilogue

Well, it has been an honor and a privilege to share my journey with you. I pray that my story sheds light on any darkness in your life. I pray that you would take heed to this warning and not drive under the influence of anything. I pray that my tribulation helps you avoid yours.

I pray that the correlation between the things that happened thousands of years ago in biblical times and my modern-day trials spark an interest in you that would cause you to pick up your Bible, read the Word, and find the same similarities to your life. The Word will give you a revelation of the things that God wants to repair in your life.

Death and life are in the power of the tongue and I pray that you would choose life by repeating this out loud: "I confess with my mouth that Jesus Christ is my Lord and Savior. I believe in my heart that God raised Him from the dead" (Romans 10:9). I pray that you confessed that out loud and that you meant it because if you did you are now saved! God bless you.

ABOUT THE AUTHOR

Rodney Wright grew up in Inglewood, California in a household plagued with poverty, violence, and drug addiction. As a youth he focused on basketball and music to escape the lure of the gang culture prevalent in Los Angeles. He attended Mt. San Antonio College before beginning his career at Southern California Gas Company where he worked for over 19 years and became a senior Commercial Technician.

Rodney currently works as a Commercial Technician in Burbank, California. He also invests in real estate properties in lower income areas to help revitalize the communities. He devotes his time to teaching Bible studies to his family and friends and also as a Connect Group leader at the church where he and his wife are members, Hope's House Ministries in Granada Hills, California. Rodney's favorite pastime is volunteering as a youth basketball coach for 12–14-year-olds. Rodney has 4 daughters and a bonus son with his wife, Cha'Ticia.

Connect with Rodney.
✉ Mrrdwright@gmail.com
◉ @thewrightwaybooks
❋ @Issa Wrightway

www.ingramcontent.com/pod-product-compliance
Lightning Source LLC
Chambersburg PA
CBHW062225080426
42734CB00010B/2033